EASY
KNITS
FOR
Beautiful
YARNS

TOBY ROXANE BARNA

EASY KNITS FOR *Beautiful* YARNS

- - - - - - - - - -

21 Shawls, Hats,
Sweaters & More
Designed to Showcase
Special Yarns

- - - - - - - - - -

STACKPOLE
BOOKS

Guilford, Connecticut

TOBY ROXANE BARNA

Published by Stackpole Books
An imprint of The Rowman & Littlefield Publishing Group, Inc.
4501 Forbes Blvd., Ste. 200
Lanham, MD 20706
www.stackpolebooks.com

Distributed by NATIONAL BOOK NETWORK
800-462-6420

Model photography by Gale Zucker
Technique photography by Chad Ferber

We have made every effort to ensure the accuracy and completeness of these instructions. We cannot, however, be responsible for human error, typographical mistakes, or variations in individual work.

British Library Cataloguing in Publication Information available

Library of Congress Cataloging-in-Publication Data available

Names: Barna, Toby Roxane, author.
Title: Easy knits for beautiful yarns : 21 shawls, hats, sweaters & more
   designed to showcase special yarns / Toby Roxane Barna.
Description: First edition. | Guilford, Connecticut : Stackpole Books,
   [2020] | Summary: "Gorgeous yarns abound for the knitter, but sometimes
   the color variations can make it difficult to find patterns that allow
   the yarn to shine. With this in mind, Toby Roxane Barna designed all of
   the pieces in this book—hats, shawls, mittens, sweaters, and more—to
   let the yarn be the main feature" — Provided by publisher.
Identifiers: LCCN 2020001318 (print) | LCCN 2020001319 (ebook) | ISBN
   9780811738590 (paperback) | ISBN 9780811768566 (epub)
Subjects: LCSH: Knitting—Patterns. | Knitwear. | Yarn.
Classification: LCC TT825 .B29573 2020 (print) | LCC TT825 (ebook) | DDC
   746.43/2—dc23
LC record available at https://lccn.loc.gov/2020001318
LC ebook record available at https://lccn.loc.gov/2020001319

♾™ The paper used in this publication meets the minimum requirements of
American National Standard for Information Sciences—Permanence of Paper
for Printed Library Materials, ANSI/NISO Z39.48-1992.

First Edition

Contents

Patterns

Introduction

If you're like many new knitters, you go into your local yarn shop or browse yarn websites and you feel overwhelmed. You're drawn to beautiful yarns, but you aren't sure how to use them. You don't feel *qualified* to use them—after all, you've only just finished your first scarf project and you're still feeling a bit wobbly. You're just not convinced that you've *earned* it yet.

Banish this mindset forever! You are just as entitled to use beautiful yarn as any other knitter, no matter how beginning or advanced. And if, like many knitters, you love the hand-dyed and hand-painted yarns you see in your yarn shop, at fiber festivals, on Etsy, and on Ravelry,* but are at a loss as to what to do with them, look no further. This book, while geared toward the beginning knitter, is also a valuable resource for anyone who's looking for a collection of patterns to suit variegated yarns.

Contained in this book are simple, accessible patterns for the types of garments and accessories that will lay the groundwork for you to move on to more intermediate projects. Not only will they make you feel more competent as a knitter, but they'll also be the kinds of things you'll actually want to wear.

If you've ever looked at Ravelry and marveled at wonderful, difficult-looking projects and thought, "I could never do that," this book is for you. The sidebar notes will show you how these easy patterns are actually the framework for more complex designs. They'll also give you tips and tricks that will help you with patterns you knit in the future.

An item of knitwear doesn't have to be complicated to be beautiful. Here's a secret that lots of knitters know: Sometimes the yarn speaks for itself. Sometimes the simplest patterns are the ones that showcase the yarn to its best advantage. Let the yarn do the work!

---

* Ravelry (www.ravelry.com) is an incredible resource, and all knitters should be aware of its many advantages. It's free to sign up, and once you do, you'll be able to do things such as see what other people have made with a specific yarn, join groups of people who share your interests (both knitting and non-knitting related), and keep track of your yarn stash. These are just a few of the ways to use Ravelry—join today! (I'm not getting paid to say this. I really feel this strongly. Talk to any member who's familiar with the site, and you'll hear the same thing.)

How to Use This Book

The patterns in this book are organized according to difficulty, starting with the easiest. All the patterns are suitable for relative beginners, but each uses progressively more skills. I've included a heading at the beginning of each pattern that lists the skills used in that project. Assuming you already know how to cast on, knit, purl, and bind off, every other technique that will appear in the pattern is listed.

In the past, you may have encountered "Difficulty Ratings." In my experience, difficulty ratings aren't always accurate. Some knitters might find the "M1" increase much easier than the cable cast-on, while others may not. The "Skills Used" heading eliminates this issue. This way, you can tell from the start exactly which techniques you'll be tackling in any given project—and plan accordingly.

Learning new techniques is how we grow as knitters, but make sure not to overwhelm yourself. As you're choosing your next project, select one that has no more than one or two skills that are new to you. I've also included photo tutorials for several techniques that may be unfamiliar, and don't forget that YouTube is your friend! By typing the name of a stitch pattern or technique into YouTube's search bar, you'll find dozens (at least!) of videos that show you exactly what you need to know. One of the great things about YouTube videos is that you can pause them whenever you want, and you can watch them over and over again without the teacher ever losing patience.

It's also important to remember that making mistakes is part of how we learn. Ripping things out is part of the process. Never think of mistakes you've made and had to rip out as time wasted—it was time spent *learning*. But also keep in mind that not all mistakes are worth ripping out. My rule of thumb is that if you can't see the problem from more than two feet away and it's not causing a structural issue (i.e., a dropped stitch that will unravel), the decision of whether to rip it out is up to you. It's unlikely that anyone besides you will ever notice it, and if they *do* notice the mistake and point it out, you have my permission to smack them.

Above all, don't forget that knitting is supposed to be relaxing and *fun*. There's nothing wrong with sticking to projects and techniques you feel comfortable with.

A Note on Choosing Colors

All of the patterns in this book are designed to show off colorful hand-dyed yarns, but don't feel like you *must* use the yarn suggested in the pattern. Part of the beauty of hand knitting is that you get to choose whatever yarn you want to use (within reason—gauge is important) and see how your choice makes your project truly one of a kind.

Many of the yarns that are most appealing to knitters are variegated. This means that they aren't one single color—they're a blend of several different colors. Normally, choosing a pattern to knit with this type of yarn can be tricky: complicated stitch patterns like lace or cables can be obscured by wild colors, and all the work you put into your project won't show. However, this book is your ticket to go crazy! All the patterns, including the ones shown in more subtle, solid colors (such as the Abigail Shawl on page 31), will look equally stunning in a wild variegated yarn or in a more restrained semi-solid or tonal colorway.

If you're looking to substitute yarns for the ones used in this book, pay close attention to the gauge. The recommended needle size on the ball band isn't always the best way to decide—that needle size will give you one of several possible gauges to which that particular yarn can be knit. Consider that you would want the fabric of a sock to be on the tighter, stiffer side, while a shawl is meant to have drape and flow. For example, I used Toby Roxane Designs Contact Sport yarn for the Treehouse Socks (page 73) on a size US 2 needle and for the Hothouse Shawl (page 43) on a US 7. A better solution is to make sure that the number of yards per 3.5 oz. (100 g) is close to the yardage per 3.5 oz. (100 g) of the yarn the pattern calls for. But when it comes to color, the only limit is your imagination!

ABBREVIATIONS

BO	bind off
BOR	beginning of round
CC	contrasting color
CO	cast on
dpn(s)	double-pointed needle(s)
k	knit
k2tog	knit 2 stitches together
kfb	knit in the front and back of the same stitch
m	marker
M1	make 1 stitch (using left-hand needle, knit into the strand between next stitch and stitch just worked)
M1L	make 1 left-leaning knit stitch (using left-hand needle, pick up strand between next stitch and stitch just worked from front to back, knit into back of stitch)
M1R	make 1 right-leaning knit stitch (using left-hand needle, pick up strand between next stitch and stitch just worked from back to front, knit into front of stitch)
M1Lp	make 1 left-leaning purl stitch (using left-hand needle, pick up strand between next stitch and stitch just made from back to front, purl into front of stitch)
M1Rp	make 1 right-leaning purl stitch (using left-hand needle, pick up strand between next stitch and stitch just made from front to back, purl into back of stitch)
MC	main color
p	purl
p2tog	purl 2 stitches together
pm	place marker
rnd(s)	round(s)
RS	right side
ssk	slip, slip, knit
slm	slip marker
st(s)	stitch(es)
tbl	through the back loop
w&t	wrap and turn
WS	wrong side
yo	yarn over

Technicolor
Dream Cowl

This easy cowl knits up quickly in a bulky yarn; it also makes a great last-minute gift! Using one skein of each color, it's a great opportunity to have fun choosing coordinating colors, along with some great statement buttons.

Pro tip: If you want the stripes to really stand out, make sure to choose two colors that are very different from each other. If you choose two colors that are similar—for example, a variegated plus a semi-solid that appears in the variegated—you won't see the stripes as much. Instead, it will appear almost as one color.

Materials

YARN: Toby Roxane Designs Cozy Bulky (80% superwash merino, 20% nylon; 76 yd./69 m per 3.5 oz./100 g)
- » Technicolor Dream: 1 skein for Color A
- » African Violet: 1 skein for Color B

NEEDLES: Size US 15/10 mm circular needle, 24 in./60 cm or longer

NOTIONS: 2 large buttons (1¾–2 in./44–50 mm)

Gauge

9 sts and 24 rows = 4 in./10 cm over garter stitch

Finished Measurements

Circumference (buttoned): 42 in./107 cm
Height: 5 in./12.5 cm

Skills Used

- » Yarn over increases
- » K2tog decreases

Directions

Using Color A, CO 100 sts.

STRIPE PATTERN:
Knit 2 rows with Color A.
Knit 2 rows with Color B.
Continue alternating colors every other row.

At the same time:
When you have worked a total of 8 rows (4 stripes), work
    buttonhole as follows:
Next row: K3, yo, k2tog, knit to end.
Next row: Knit.
Work 8 more rows (4 more stripes), and then work button-
    hole again.

*Note: First buttonhole rows are worked with
Color A; second are worked with Color B.*

Continue in pattern for 8 more rows (4 more stripes), end-
    ing with Color B.
BO all sts.

Sew buttons to edge of cowl, opposite buttonholes.

Weave in ends, block if desired, and wear proudly!

LILAC LEG WARMERS

Leg warmers aren't just for ballerinas (or the 1980s)!
These fun, spat-like leg warmers are a great chance to go
scouting for some vintage buttons.

Materials

YARN: Toby Roxane Designs Velvet Aran (100% superwash merino; 181 yd./166 m per 3.5 oz./100 g)
» Lilac: 2 skeins

NEEDLES: Size US 7/4.5 mm straight or circular needles (any length)

NOTIONS: Locking stitch markers (optional), tapestry needle

Gauge

16 sts and 30 rows = 4 in./10 cm over 2x2 ribbing, firmly stretched (as worn)

Finished Measurements

Due to the very stretchy nature of ribbing, this leg warmer can fit a wide variety of leg circumferences. As written, these will fit leg circumferences 12–16 in./30–41 cm. If your calf circumference is significantly smaller, subtract 4 sts from the CO. Likewise, if your calf is significantly larger, add 4 sts to the CO.

Skills Used

» Yarn over increases
» P2tog decreases

Directions

CO 54 sts.

Work in 2x2 ribbing ([k2, p2] to end) for 4 rows.

Tip:

When you reach the end of the Buttonhole Row, you may want to hang a locking stitch marker from your last **knit stitch** in the row (this will be the third-to-last stitch on your needle). Doing so will help you mark where to sew the buttons on later.

Buttonhole Row: K2, p2tog, yo, [k2, p2] to end.

Continue working in 2x2 ribbing, repeating Buttonhole Row every 10th row until you have worked a total of 7 Buttonhole Rows (or until work reaches desired length).

Work in 2x2 ribbing for 4 more rows.

BO all sts in pattern.

Using the locking stitch markers as a guide, sew buttons to edge of leg warmer to correspond to buttonholes.

Weave in all ends, block if desired, and wear proudly!

PISTACHIO
BABY BLANKET

It's always good to have a go-to baby blanket pattern on hand when you need a baby gift. Most new parents don't have the time to care for hand-knits the way we'd recommend, so it's not a bad idea to pick up some inexpensive, machine-washable and -dryable yarn at a craft store. They have some great options these days!

Materials

YARN: Caron Cakes (80% acrylic, 20% wool; 383 yd./350 m per 7 oz./200 g)
>> Pistachio: 2 balls
NEEDLES: Size US 7/4.5 mm circular needles, 16 in./40 cm and 24 in./60 cm, and double-pointed needles (1 set)
NOTIONS: Stitch markers (9 of one color or type, plus 1 to mark beginning of round), tapestry needle

Gauge

18 sts and 26 rnds = 4 in./10 cm over stockinette stitch, after blocking

Finished Measurements

36 in./91.5 cm in diameter

Skills Used

>> Joining/working in the round
>> Using double-pointed needles
>> Yarn over increases
>> Kfb increases

Directions

BODY

Using dpns, CO 5 sts. Being careful not to twist your sts, place beginning-of-rnd (BOR) marker, and join to work in the round.

Rnd 1: Kfb all sts—10 sts.

Rnd 2: [K1, pm] to last st, k1.

Rnd 3: [K1, yo, slm] to end—20 sts.

Rnd 4: Knit.

Rnd 5: [Knit to m, yo, slm] to end—10 sts increased.

Repeat Rnds 4 and 5 until work measures 15 in./38 cm from center (the radius of the circle), ending with a Rnd 5.

Tip:

As your stitch count increases, I recommend arranging your stitches on the double-pointed needles so that the ends of each needle are in the middle of a section (i.e., not separated by a marker). This way, you won't lose your yarn overs!

When you have more stitches than fit comfortably around your dpns, switch to the 16 in./40 cm circular needle, and then the 24 in./60 cm circular needle.

BORDER

Rnd 1: Purl.

Rnd 2: [Knit to m, yo, slm] to end—10 sts increased.

Repeat Rnds 1 and 2 until Border measures 3 in./7.5 cm, ending with a Rnd 1.

BO all sts **loosely** (you may want to use a needle a few sizes bigger).

Note:

It's very important that you bind off loosely because of the stretchy nature of garter stitch. If the bind-off isn't loose enough to allow the blanket to stretch a little, it may not lie flat.

Weave in ends, block, and wrap up a baby!

KATE'S
MOSS HAT

As soon as this hat came off my needles, it became one of my all-time favorites. The Mohair Silk carried along with the Beautilitarian DK gives the fabric an ethereal halo of fuzz (and some extra warmth). Feel free to experiment by using a skein of Mohair Silk that's a different color from the Beautilitarian DK—the color of the mohair will blend with the other yarn and shift the hue in a subtle, beautiful way.

Materials

YARN: Toby Roxane Designs Beautilitarian DK (100% superwash merino; 250 yd./229 m per 3.5 oz./100 g)
  » Kate's Moss: 1 skein
Toby Roxane Designs Mohair Silk (70% kid mohair, 30% silk; 458 yd./419 m per 1.75 oz./50 g)
  » Kate's Moss: 1 skein
NEEDLES:
  » Size US 5/3.75 mm circular needle, 16 in./40 cm
  » Size US 8/5 mm circular needle, 16 in./40 cm, and double-pointed needles (1 set)
NOTIONS: Stitch marker (1), tapestry needle, pom-pom (optional)

Gauge

18 sts and 32 rnds = 4 in./10 cm over garter stitch on larger needles with both yarns held together

Finished Measurements

Brim circumference is 17½ in./44.5 cm, unstretched. Hat will fit head circumference up to 23 in./58 cm.

Skills Used

  » Joining/knitting in the round
  » K2tog decreases
  » Using double-pointed needles
  » M1 increases

Directions

BRIM

Using smaller circular needle and both yarns held
together, CO 88 sts. Being careful not to twist sts, pm
and join to work in the round.
Establish 2x2 ribbing: [K2, p2] to end.
Repeat this rnd until ribbing measures 1½ in./4 cm.

BODY

Switch to larger circular needle.
Increase rnd: [K10, M1] to last 8 sts, k8—96 sts.
Next rnd: Purl.
Next rnd: Knit.
Repeat last 2 rnds until work measures 4½ in./11.5 cm
from top of ribbing, ending with a purl rnd.

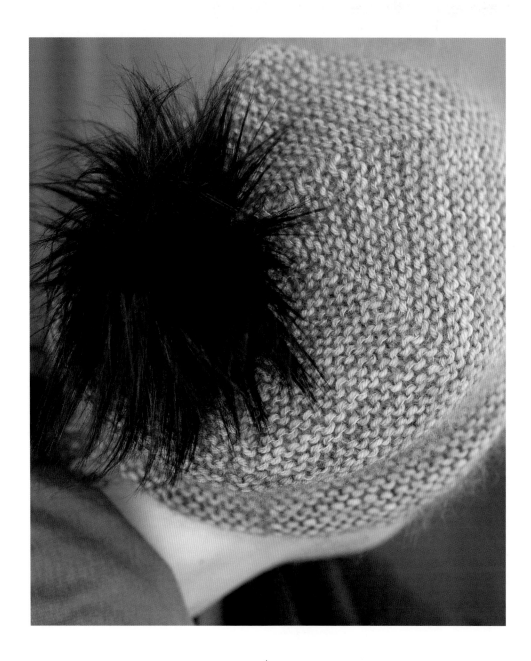

CROWN

(Switch to dpns when sts no longer fit comfortably around circular needle.)

Rnd 1: [K14, k2tog] to end—90 sts.

Rnd 2 and all even-numbered rnds until otherwise instructed: Purl.

Rnd 3: [K13, k2tog] to end—84 sts.

Rnd 5: [K12, k2tog] to end—78 sts.

Rnd 7: [K11, k2tog] to end—72 sts.

Rnd 9: [K10, k2tog] to end—66 sts.

Rnd 11: [K9, k2tog] to end—60 sts.

Rnd 13: [K8, k2tog] to end—54 sts.

Rnd 15: [K7, k2tog] to end—48 sts.

Rnd 17: [K6, k2tog] to end—42 sts.

Rnd 19: [K5, k2tog] to end—36 sts.

Rnd 21: [K4, k2tog] to end—30 sts.

Rnd 22: [P3, p2tog] to end—24 sts.

Rnd 23: [K2tog] to end—12 sts.

Break yarn, leaving a tail approximately 10 in./25 cm long. Using a tapestry needle, thread tail through all 12 remaining sts and pull tight. Weave in end on inside of hat. Sew (or tie) on a pom-pom if desired.

Weave in any remaining ends, block if desired, and wear proudly!

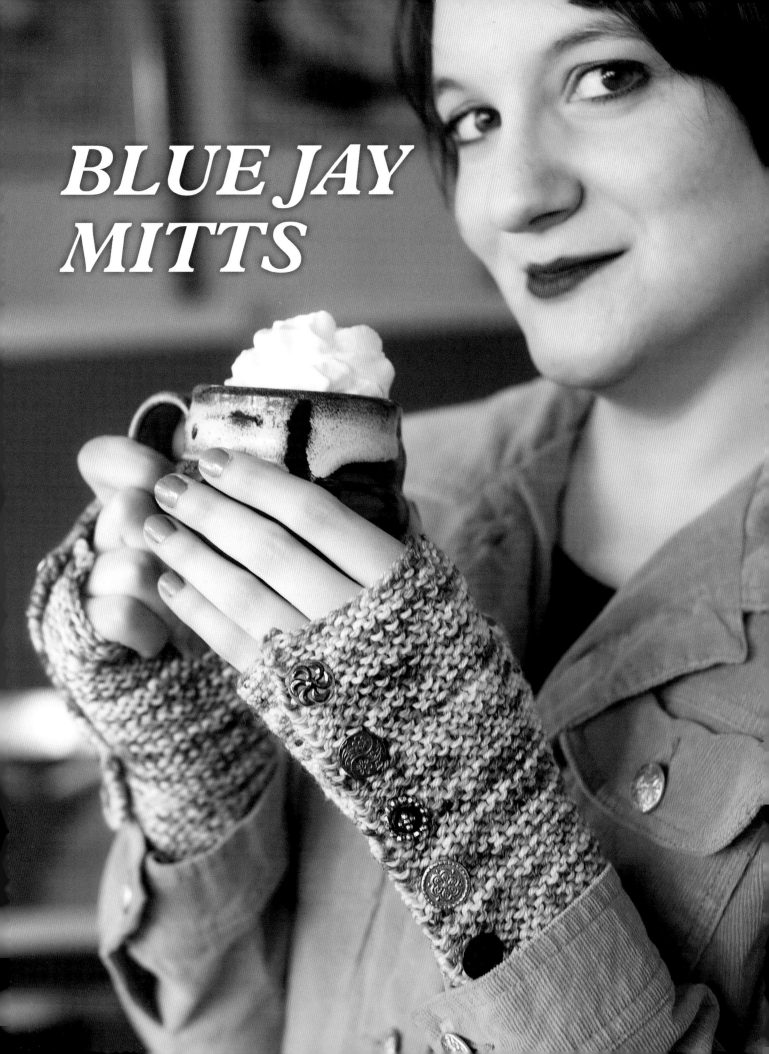

BLUE JAY MITTS

Fingerless mitts keep your hands warm but still allow you to use your fingers to unlock the door or send a text message, and these are a perfect pair to start with. They're worked flat (as opposed to in the round) and closed with buttons at the sides. Another great opportunity to raid the button jar!

Materials

YARN: Toby Roxane Designs Polwarth DK (100% superwash Polwarth wool; 252 yd./230 m per 3.5 oz./ 100 g)

» Blue Jay: 1 skein

NEEDLES: Size US 7/4.5 mm straight or circular needles (any length)

NOTIONS: Stitch markers (2), locking stitch markers (5), 10 small buttons (½–¾ in./1–2 cm), tapestry needle

Gauge

20 sts and 42 rows = 4 in./10 cm over garter stitch

Finished Measurements

Mitts measure 7½ in./19 cm around, unbuttoned, and 5¾ in./14.5 cm in length. Finished circumference is adjustable; place buttons nearer to or farther from the edge of the mitt to achieve desired fit.

Skills Used

» K2tog decreases
» Yarn over increases
» M1L/M1R increases
» Backward loop cast-on

Tips:

When you knit the first stitch of a row, pull it tight. This will close the loop made by the last stitch of the previous row and neaten up your edge (don't pull it *too* tight—just enough to make a nice, even edge along the side of your work). This is the only stitch you're allowed to pull, though! In general, you don't want to pull your stitches too tight. They should be able to scoot comfortably along your needle.

I recommend hanging locking stitch markers to mark button placement. See page 8 (Lilac Leg Warmers Tip). I also recommend hanging a locking stitch marker to differentiate the right and wrong sides. See page 34 (Abigail Shawl Tip).

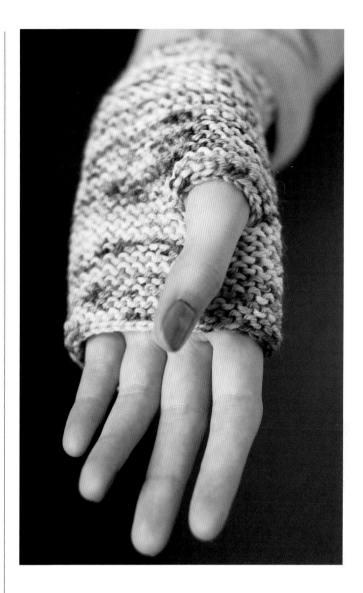

Directions

RIGHT MITT

CO 38 sts.
Knit 8 rows.
Buttonhole Row (RS): K2, k2tog, yo, knit to end.
Knit 11 rows, and then work Buttonhole Row once more.
Knit 1 row.

Work thumb gusset as follows:
Row 1 (RS): K19, pm, M1R, k1, M1L, pm, knit to end—40 sts.
Row 2 (WS): Knit.
Row 3: Knit to m, slm, M1R, knit to m, M1L, slm, knit to end—2 sts increased.
Rows 4–10: Work Rows 2 and 3 three more times, and then repeat Row 2 once more—48 sts.
Row 11 (RS—buttonhole): K2, k2tog, yo , knit to m, remove m, BO 11 thumb sts, remove m, knit to end—37 sts.
Row 12 (WS): Knit to gap, CO 1 st using the backward loop method, knit to end—38 sts.
Knit 10 rows, and then work Buttonhole Row.
Knit 11 rows, and then work Buttonhole Row.
Knit 4 rows.
BO all sts.

LEFT MITT

CO 38 sts.
Knit 8 rows.
Buttonhole Row (RS): Knit to last 4 sts, yo, k2tog, k2.
Knit 11 rows, and then work Buttonhole Row once more.
Knit 1 row.

Work thumb gusset as follows:
Row 1 (RS): K18, pm, M1R, k1, M1L, pm, knit to end—40 sts.
Row 2 (WS): Knit.
Row 3: Knit to m, slm, M1R, knit to m, M1L, slm, knit to end—2 sts increased.
Rows 4–10: Work Rows 2 and 3 three more times, and then repeat Row 2 once more—48 sts.
Row 11 (RS—buttonhole): Knit to m, remove m, BO 11 thumb sts, remove m, knit to last 4 sts, yo, k2tog, k2—37 sts.

Row 12 (WS): Knit to gap, CO 1 st using the backward loop method, knit to end—38 sts.
Knit 10 rows, and then work Buttonhole Row.
Knit 11 rows, and then work Buttonhole Row.
Knit 4 rows.
BO all sts.

Sew buttons opposite buttonholes, placing them an appropriate distance from the edge to achieve desired size.

Weave in ends, block if desired, and wear proudly!

SUMMER STORM SHAWL

Shawls are some of the most popular items to knit for a number of reasons: Since they don't need to fit a specific body in a specific way, gauge is not as important as it is for garments like sweaters. With shawls, there is minimal finishing involved (no seams to sew, not many ends to weave in), and they're usually small enough to be portable—toss the project in your bag and knit on the train, in waiting rooms, on the bus . . . pretty much anywhere!

With its simple stockinette stitch body and garter stitch border, Summer Storm is the perfect project to dip your toes into shawl knitting.

Materials

YARN: Toby Roxane Designs Elegance Fingering (80% superwash merino, 10% cashmere, 10% nylon; 435 yd./400 m per 3.5 oz./100 g)
>> Summer Storm: 1 skein
NEEDLES: Size US 6/4 mm circular needle, 24 in./60 cm or longer
NOTIONS: Stitch markers (2), tapestry needle

Gauge

23 sts and 36 rows = 4 in./10 cm over stockinette stitch, after blocking

Finished Measurements

50 in./127 cm across, 19½ in./49.5 cm deep at center

Skills Used

>> Garter tab cast-on (See tutorial on page 24.)
>> Yarn over increases
>> K2tog tbl (through back loop)

Directions

Garter tab CO: CO 3 sts.

Knit 6 rows. At the end of the last row, do not turn work. Rotate work 90 degrees clockwise, pick up and knit 3 sts along side edge, and then rotate work 90 degrees again, pick up and knit 3 sts along CO edge—9 sts.

Setup row (WS): K3, yo, [p1, pm] twice, p1, yo, k3—11 sts.

Note:

If you've ever knitted a top-down shawl before, it might have had the edge yarn overs only on right-side rows. I like to put yarn overs on the edges of both right- *and* wrong-side rows because I find it makes the shawl a shallower triangle shape—almost a heart shape—that stays on your shoulders no matter how you wear it.

BODY

Row 1 (RS): K3, yo, knit to m, yo, slm, k1, slm, yo, knit to last 3 sts, yo, k3—4 sts increased.

Row 2 (WS): K3, yo, purl to last 3 sts, yo, k3—2 sts increased.

Repeat Rows 1 and 2 until work measures 9 in./23 cm (or desired length) along center spine.

GARTER STITCH BORDER

Row 1 (RS): K3, yo, knit to m, yo, slm, k1, slm, yo, knit to last 3 sts, yo, k3—4 sts increased.

Row 2 (WS): K3, yo, knit to last 3 sts, yo, k3—2 sts increased.

Repeat Rows 1 and 2 until garter section measures 5 in./13 cm (or desired length).

BO loosely as follows: *K2tog tbl, slip st from right-hand needle back onto left-hand needle. Repeat from * until 1 st remains. Break yarn and pull through.

Weave in ends, block, and wear proudly!

TUTORIAL: GARTER TAB CAST-ON

1. Cast on three stitches and knit six rows as the Summer Storm Shawl pattern instructs. If you're making a different shawl, check the pattern for the correct number of stitches to cast on and number of rows to knit. Though the pattern numbers may be different, the technique is the same.

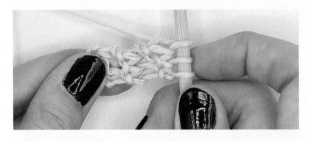

2. Keeping your needle in your right hand after you finish knitting the sixth row, rotate your work so that the left edge is now at the top (your needle should be pointing straight up).

3. Insert the tip of your right-hand needle under the horizontal strand closest to the needle.

4. Wrap the yarn and pull through. You have now picked up one stitch along the side edge.

5. Pick up a stitch through the middle strand, and the last one.

6. You should now have six stitches on your needle.

7. Now, rotate your work again so that the cast-on edge is at the top (again, your needle should now be pointing straight up).

8. Insert your right-hand needle into the corner of your work (where the tail is coming from) and pull a stitch through.

9. Insert your needle under the middle strand of the cast-on edge, pull a stitch through.

10. Finally, insert your needle under a strand in the corner of your work and pull a stitch through. (**Note:** This last stitch can be fussy. Don't worry too much about where you're inserting the needle; the goal is to pick up those three stitches along the cast-on edge.)

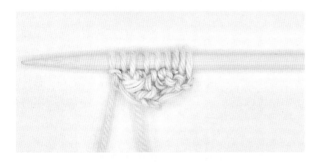

11. You should now have nine stitches on your needle. You're ready to begin Row 1 of the pattern!

KAATERSKILL SHAWL

With its starfish-like shape, the Kaaterskill Shawl may seem like a big leap in difficulty from the Summer Storm Shawl, but it's really not—the only real difference is that it has three center "spines" instead of just one. After it's finished, you'll want to block this shawl (soak it in water, wool wash optional) and pin it out to accentuate the points.

Materials

YARN: Toby Roxane Designs Beautilitarian DK (100% superwash merino; 250 yd./229 m per 3.5 oz./100 g)
- » Kaaterskill: 2 skeins for Main Color
- » Auburn: 1 skein for Contrasting Color

NEEDLES: Size US 8/5 mm circular needle, 24 in./60 cm or longer

NOTIONS: Stitch markers (6), tapestry needle

Note:

In this shawl, the Contrasting Color is only used for the bind-off. This means that you do not necessarily need to have a whole skein of that color on hand—it's a perfect opportunity to use scraps left over from another project! Just make sure you have at least 0.2–0.4 oz./5–10 g.

Gauge

18 sts and 30 rows = 4 in./10 cm over stockinette stitch, after blocking

Finished Measurements

49 in./124.5 cm wide, 22 in./56 cm deep along center spines

Skills Used

- » Garter tab cast-on (See tutorial on page 24; note that the number of stitches in this pattern is different, but the technique is the same.)
- » Yarn over increases
- » K2tog tbl (through back loop)

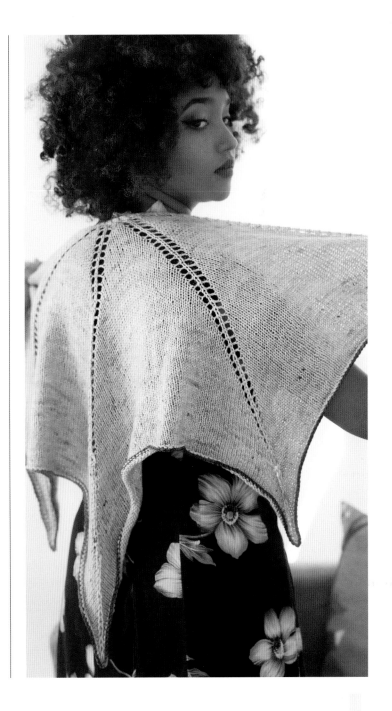

Directions

Garter tab CO: Using MC, CO 2 sts.

Knit 14 rows. At the end of the last row, do not turn. Rotate work 90 degrees clockwise, pick up and knit 7 sts along side edge, and then rotate work 90 degrees again, pick up and knit 2 sts along CO edge—11 sts.

Setup row (WS): K2, yo, [p1, pm] six times, p1, yo, k2—13 sts.

Row 1 (RS): K2, [yo, knit to m, yo, slm, k1, slm] three times, yo, knit to last 2 sts, yo, k2—8 sts increased.

Row 2: K2, yo, purl to last 2 sts, yo, k2—2 sts increased.

Repeat Rows 1 and 2 until work measures 16 in./40.5 cm, measuring along one of the center "spines," ending with a WS row.

Row 3 (RS): As Row 1.

Row 4 (WS): K2, [yo, purl to m, yo, slm, p1, slm] three times, yo, purl to last 2 sts, yo, k2—8 sts increased.

Repeat Rows 3 and 4 until work measures 21 in./53.5 cm, ending with a WS row.

Switch to CC.

BO loosely as follows: *K2tog tbl, slip st from right-hand needle back onto left-hand needle. Repeat from * until 1 st remains. Break yarn and pull through.

Weave in ends, block, and wear proudly!

A NOTE ON BLOCKING

Blocking is one of my favorite magic tricks of knitting. While it's true that some things don't usually need to be blocked (hats, mitts), most knitted items do benefit from a good wet blocking.

For sweaters, you can get away with steaming. I highly recommend investing in a quality steamer—you can get a good one for not much money. However, if you're careful, you can also use an iron. One method is to set the iron on a very hot setting, with steam; hover the iron an inch or two above your sweater and blast it with steam.

Another thing you can do is take a damp towel (fresh from the washing machine is a good level of moisture), lay it over your sweater, and set your iron to a very hot setting. Hover the iron over the towel so that it's just barely touching the nap of the towel. This will create a "steam chamber" under the towel and force the steam to penetrate the wool.

With shawls, a good wet blocking is ideal. To do this, prepare a tub of cool or lukewarm water. Many companies now make a no-rinse wool wash, and you can add a teaspoon or two of this product to the water. Submerge your shawl, and squeeze it under the water to release as many air bubbles as possible. Let the shawl sit for a while to really let as much water into the fiber as you can. After five to ten minutes, take the shawl out. Try to support the entire weight of the shawl, kind of like you'd hold a baby, so that you don't have any bits trailing down into the water. Squeeze out as much water as you can *without wringing*—wringing will distort your stitches and cause your beautiful shawl to hang a bit crooked. Lay the wet shawl on a towel, lay a second towel over it, and roll them up. I recommend standing on the towel roll (barefoot) to squeeze out even more water. At this point, your shawl should be damp, not soaking wet.

Now, lay your shawl out. I like to use foam-rubber interlocking floor mats—you can find them in the flooring department at your local hardware store. Pin out the top edge of the shawl, keeping the lines as straight as you can. Then pin out the points of the shawl. Some shawls, like the one pictured, have many points to pin, while the Kaaterskill Shawl just has three.

Let your shawl dry. When it's thoroughly dry, unpin it, and admire your shawl's perfect shape!

ABIGAIL SHAWL

Knitted in an aran weight yarn (aran is slightly heavier than worsted), this shawl knits up quickly. It's the perfect thing to wrap up in on a cozy winter evening.

Materials

YARN: Toby Roxane Designs Velvet Aran (100% superwash merino; 181 yd./166 m per 3.5 oz./100 g)
  » Abigail: 3 skeins

NEEDLES:
  » Size US 8/5 mm circular needle, 24 in./60 cm or longer
  » Size US 11/8mm circular needle, 32 in./80 cm or longer

NOTIONS: Stitch markers (2), tapestry needle

Gauge

14 sts and 30 rows = 4 in./10 cm over garter stitch on smaller needles, after blocking

Finished Measurements

71 in./180 cm wide, 23 in./58.5 cm deep at center, after blocking

Skills Used

  » Garter tab cast-on (See tutorial on page 24; note that the number of stitches in this pattern is different, but the technique is the same.)
  » Yarn over increases
  » Kfb increases
  » K2tog tbl (through back loop)

Directions

Tip:

> I recommend hanging a locking stitch marker (the kind that looks like a plastic safety pin) from the **right side** of your work in order to differentiate it from the wrong side. This will help you remember on which rows to do the center kfb increases!

Garter tab CO: CO 2 sts.

Knit 6 rows. At the end of the last row, do not turn work. Rotate work 90 degrees clockwise, pick up and knit 3 sts along side edge, and then rotate work 90 degrees again, pick up and knit 2 sts along CO edge—7 sts.

Setup row (WS): K2, yo, [k1, pm] twice, k1, yo, k2—9 sts.

BODY

Row 1 (RS): K2, yo, knit to 1 st before m, kfb, slm, k1, slm, kfb, knit to last 2 sts, yo, k2—4 sts increased.

Row 2 (WS): K2, yo, knit to last 2 sts, yo, k2—2 sts increased.

Repeat Rows 1 and 2 until work measures 16 in./40.5 cm (or desired length) along center spine, ending with a WS row.

BORDER

Switch to larger circular needle.

Row 1 (RS): K2, yo, [k10, kfb] until you have fewer than 10 sts before m, knit to 1 st before m, kfb, slm, k1, slm, kfb, [k10, kfb] until you have fewer than 12 sts remaining, knit to last 2 sts, yo, k2.

Row 2 (WS): K2, yo, knit to last 2 sts, yo, k2—2 sts increased.

Row 3: K2, yo, knit to 1 st before m, kfb, slm, k1, slm, kfb, knit to last 2 sts, yo, k2—4 sts increased.

Repeat Rows 2 and 3 until Border measures 3 in./7.5 cm (or desired length).

BO loosely as follows: *K2tog tbl, slip st from right-hand needle back onto left-hand needle. Repeat from * until 1 st remains. Break yarn and pull through.

Weave in ends, block, and wear proudly!

MOONLIGHT HAT

This hat is the perfect unisex watch cap. Make one for everyone you know!

Materials

YARN: Toby Roxane Designs Polwarth DK (100% superwash Polwarth wool; 252 yd./230 m per 3.5 oz./ 100 g)

» Moonlight: 1 skein

NEEDLES: Size US 5/3.75 mm circular needle, 16 in./40 cm, and double-pointed needles (1 set)

NOTIONS: Stitch marker (1), tapestry needle

Gauge

28 sts and 33 rnds = 4 in./10 cm over 2x2 ribbing, slightly stretched

Finished Measurements

Due to the very stretchy nature of ribbing, this hat will fit a variety of head circumferences. It's shown on my head, which measures about 21 in./54 cm.

Skills Used

» Joining/working in the round
» Using double-pointed needles
» P2tog/k2tog decreases

Directions

Using circular needle, CO 120 sts. Being careful not to twist
   sts, pm and join to work in the round.

Establish 2x2 ribbing: [K2, p2] to end.

Work in 2x2 ribbing until work measures 9 in./23 cm.

Work crown decreases as follows, switching to dpns when
   sts no longer fit comfortably around circular needle:

Rnd 1: ([K2, p2] twice, k2, p2tog) to end—110 sts.

Rnd 2: ([K2, p2] twice, k2, p1) to end.

Rnd 3: (K2, p2, k2, p2tog, k2, p1) to end—100 sts.

Rnd 4: (K2, p2, [k2, p1] twice) to end.

Rnd 5: (K2, p2tog, [k2, p1] twice) to end—90 sts.

Rnd 6: [K2, p1] to end.

Rnd 7: ([K2, p1] twice, k2tog, p1) to end—80 sts.

Rnd 8: ([K2, p1] twice, k1, p1) to end.

Rnd 9: ([K2tog, p1] twice, k1, p1) to end—60 sts.

Rnd 10: [K2tog] to end—30 sts.

Rnd 11: [K2tog] to end—15 sts.

Break yarn, leaving a 12 in./30 cm tail. Using a tapestry
   needle, thread tail through all remaining sts and pull
   tight. Weave in end on inside of hat.

Weave in any remaining ends, block if desired, and wear
   proudly!

BABY MOONLIGHT HAT

This is a baby-sized version of the original Moonlight Hat. It makes a perfect baby gift!

Materials

YARN: Toby Roxane Designs Contact Sport (100% superwash merino; 328 yd./300 m per 3.5 oz./100 g)

» Nightgown: 1 skein

NEEDLES: Size US 2/2.75 mm circular needle, 16 in./40 cm, and double-pointed needles (1 set)

NOTIONS: Stitch marker (1), tapestry needle

Gauge

36 sts and 42 rnds = 4 in./10 cm over 2x2 ribbing, slightly stretched

Finished Measurements

Due to the very stretchy nature of ribbing, this hat will fit a variety of head circumferences. It's shown on a baby whose head measures 18 in./46 cm and will comfortably fit heads a few inches/centimeters smaller or larger.

Skills Used

» Joining/working in the round
» Using double-pointed needles
» K2tog/p2tog decreases

Directions

Using circular needle, CO 88 sts.

Being careful not to twist sts, pm and join to work in the round.

Establish 2x2 ribbing: [K2, p2] to end.

Work in ribbing as established until hat measures 7 in./ 18 cm.

Work crown decreases as follows, switching to dpns when sts no longer fit comfortably around circular needle.

Rnd 1: [K2, p2, k2, p2tog] to end—77 sts.

Rnds 2 and 3: [K2, p2, k2, p1] to end.

Rnd 4: [K2, p2tog, k2, p1] to end—66 sts.

Rnds 5 and 6: [K2, p1] to end.

Rnd 7: [K2, p1, k2tog, p1] to end—55 sts.

Rnds 8 and 9: [K2, p1, k1, p1] to end.

Rnd 10: [K2tog, p1, k1, p1] to end—44 sts.

Rnd 11: [K1, p1] to end.

Rnd 12: [K2tog, k1, p1] to end—33 sts.

Rnd 13: [K2tog, p1] to end—22 sts.

Rnd 14: [K2tog] to end—11 sts.

Break yarn, leaving a 12 in./30 cm tail. Using a tapestry needle, thread tail through all remaining sts and pull tight. Weave in end on inside of hat.

Weave in all remaining ends, block if desired, and put it on a baby!

HOTHOUSE
SHAWL

This is a lightweight, smaller shawl that can be worn in a variety of ways. The contrasting lace edging is simpler than it looks, and it's a fun opportunity to use up scraps from another project.

Materials

YARN: Toby Roxane Designs Contact Sport (100% superwash merino; 328 yd./300 m per 3.5 oz./100 g)
  » Hothouse: 1 skein for Main Color
  » Straw Into Gold: 1 skein for Contrasting Color

NEEDLES: Size US 7/4.5 mm circular needle, 24 in./60 cm or longer

NOTIONS: Stitch markers (4), tapestry needle

Note:

You don't have to buy a whole skein of yarn for the Contrasting Color if you don't want to! Since you only need enough for the edging, you can likely get away with using leftover yarn from a different project, as long as you have at least 0.5–0.7 oz./15–20 g.

Gauge

20 sts and 32 rows = 4 in./10 cm over stockinette stitch, after blocking

Finished Measurements

48 in./122 cm across, 19 in./48 cm deep along each "spine"

Skills Used

» Garter tab cast-on (See tutorial on page 24; note that the number of stitches in this pattern is different, but the technique is the same.)
» Kfb increases
» Yarn over increases
» K2tog decreases
» Cable cast-on
» Picot bind-off (See tutorial on page 46.)

Directions

Garter tab cast-on: Using MC, CO 3 sts.

Knit 10 rows. At end of last row, do not turn work. Rotate work 90 degrees clockwise, pick up and knit 5 sts along side edge. Rotate work 90 degrees again, pick up and knit 3 sts along cast-on edge—11 sts.

Row 1 (WS): K3, yo, [kfb] five times, yo, k3—18 sts.

Row 2 (RS): [K3, yo] twice, pm, k1, pm, yo, k4, yo, pm, k1, pm, [yo, k3] twice—24 sts.

Row 3: K3, yo, purl to last 3 sts, yo, k3—2 sts increased.

Row 4: K3, [yo, knit to m, yo, slm, k1, slm] twice, yo, knit to last 3 sts, yo, k3—6 sts increased.

Repeat Rows 3 and 4 an even number of times until your
work measures 13 in./33 cm, measuring along one of
the center "spines." Make sure you have an odd number
of stitches in the first and last sections (if it's even, work
1 more repeat).

Repeat Row 3 once more, so that you will end having just
completed a WS row.

EYELET BORDER

Switch to CC (you do not need to break MC—you may
carry it up the side of your work).

Row 1 (RS): K3, [yo, knit to m, yo, slm, k1, slm] twice, yo,
knit to last 3 sts, yo, k3—6 sts increased. (This is the
same as Row 4 from previous section.)

Row 2 (WS): K3, yo, knit to last 3 sts, yo, k3—2 sts
increased.

Row 3: As Row 1.

Row 4: K3, [yo, k2tog] to m, yo, slm, k1, slm, [yo, k2tog]
to m, slm, k1, slm, [yo, k2tog] to last 3 sts, yo, k3—2 sts
increased.

Row 5: As Row 1.

Row 6: As Row 2.

Break CC, switch to MC, and BO loosely as follows (Picot
Bind-Off): *BO 7 sts, slip st from right-hand needle back
to left-hand needle, using cable CO method, CO 2 sts,
repeat from * until fewer than 7 sts remain. BO all sts.

Weave in ends, block, and wear proudly!

TUTORIAL: PICOT BIND-OFF

1. Start by binding off the number of stitches the
pattern instructs.

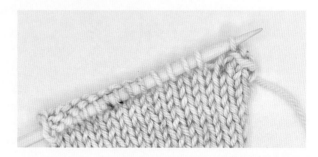

2. Slip the stitch from your right-hand needle back
onto your left-hand needle.

3. Insert your right-hand needle between the first two stitches on your left-hand needle. Wrap the yarn and pull through.

4. Place this loop on your left-hand needle. This is your first cable cast-on stitch. (*Do not* pull this stitch tight—you will want to keep it loose enough to insert your needle behind it in the next step.)

5. Insert your right-hand needle between the first two stitches on your left-hand needle.

6. Pull out a loop, as you did in Step 3.

7. Place this loop on your left-hand needle, as you did in Step 4. This is your second cast-on stitch.

8. Knit the first two stitches on your left-hand needle. Bind off one stitch by passing the second stitch on your right-hand needle over and off.

9. Knit the next stitch on your left-hand needle and bind it off in the same way. Continue to bind off the number of stitches instructed in the pattern. Repeat from Step 2.

MOUNTAIN TIME MITTS

These are your standard, serviceable, fingerless mitts. Their stockinette stitch body edged with ribbing makes them perfect for any gender, and they make a great canvas for experimenting with embroidery or applique.

Materials

YARN: Toby Roxane Designs Velvet Aran (100% superwash merino; 181 yd./166 m per 3.5 oz./100 g)

» Mountain Time: 1 skein

NEEDLES: Size US 7/4.5 mm double-pointed needles (1 set) or needle(s) for your preferred method of working small circumferences in the round

NOTIONS: Stitch markers (3), scrap yarn, tapestry needle

Gauge

20 sts and 28 rnds = 4 in./10 cm over stockinette stitch

Finished Measurements

Hand circumference: 6½ (7¼) in./16 (18) cm
To fit hand circumference: 7 (8) in./18 (20.5) cm
Length: 5¼ (5½) in./13 (14) cm

Skills Used

» Joining/working in the round
» M1R/M1L increases
» Transferring stitches to and from waste yarn

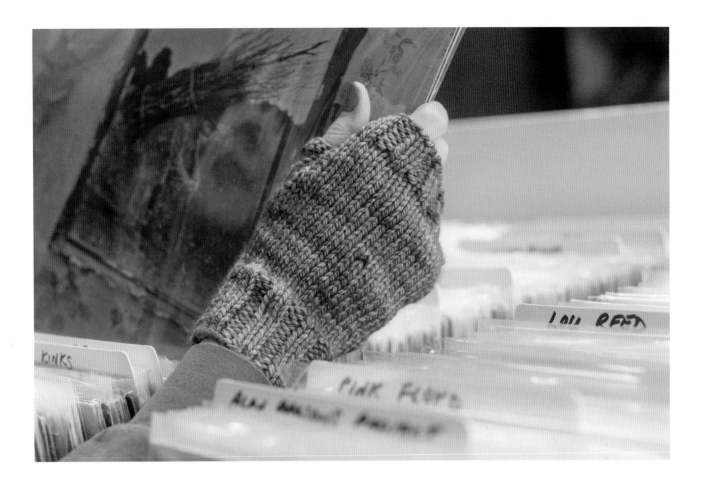

Directions (Make 2)

CO 32 (36) sts. Being careful not to twist your sts, pm, and join to work in the round.

Ribbing Rnd: [K2, p2] to end.

Repeat Ribbing Rnd for 11 more rnds (12 rnds total).

Knit 5 rnds.

Work thumb gusset as follows:

Rnd 1: K5, pm, M1R, k1, M1L, pm, knit to end—3 thumb sts; 34 (38) sts total.

Rnd 2: Knit.

Rnd 3: K5, slm, M1R, knit to m, M1L, slm, knit to end—2 sts increased.

Repeat previous 2 rnds 3 (4) more times until you have a total of 11 (13) sts between thumb markers.

Next rnd: K5, remove m, slip 11 (13) sts onto scrap yarn using a tapestry needle, remove m, using backward loop method CO 1 st, knit to end—32 (36) sts remain for hand.

Knit 5 rnds.

Work [k2 p2] ribbing for 5 rnds.

BO all sts in pattern.

THUMB

Transfer 11 (13) held thumb sts from waste yarn back onto needles. Rejoin yarn. Pick up 1 st from gap between thumb and hand at beginning of first rnd, for a total of 12 (14) sts.

Knit 2 rnds.

Next 2 rnds: [K1, p1] to end.

BO all sts in pattern.

Weave in ends, block if desired, and wear proudly!

AQUARIUS COWL

This cowl is an un-put-down-able project, and I bet you won't be able to stop at just one. It only takes one skein of a luxurious yarn, and it's the perfect opportunity to use whatever wildly variegated colorway catches your eye.

Materials

YARN: Toby Roxane Designs Super Luxe DK (75% superwash merino, 25% silk; 245 yd./300 m per 3.5 oz./ 100 g)

》 Aquarius: 1 skein

NEEDLES: Size US 7/4.5 mm circular needle, 24 in./60 cm

NOTIONS: Stitch marker (1)

Gauge

21 sts and 28 rnds = 4 in./10 cm over stockinette stitch, after blocking

Finished Measurements

Circumference: 21¾ in./54.5 cm circumference
Height: 13½ in./34.5 cm

Skills Used

》 Picot cast-on (See tutorial on page 55.)
》 Cable cast-on
》 Joining/knitting in the round
》 K2tog decreases
》 Yarn over increases
》 Picot bind-off (See tutorial on page 46.)

Directions

Work Picot CO as follows: [Cable CO 9 sts, BO 3 sts] 19 times, for a total of 114 sts. Being careful not to twist sts, pm and join to work in the round.

Rnd 1: Knit.
Rnd 2: Purl.
Rnd 3: Knit.
Rnd 4 (eyelet rnd): [K2tog, yo] to end.
Rnd 5: Knit.
Rnd 6: Purl.

Work even in stockinette stitch (knit every rnd) until work measures 12 in./30.5 cm from eyelet row, or until 0.4 oz./10 g of yarn remain, and then work Rnds 2–6 once more.

Knit 1 rnd.

Work Picot BO as follows: [BO 9 sts, cable CO 3 sts] until fewer than 9 sts remain. BO all remaining sts.

Weave in ends, block if desired, and wear proudly!

TUTORIAL: PICOT CAST-ON

1. Make a slipknot, as if you're about to begin casting on. Put the needle with the slipknot in your left hand, and insert the tip of your right-hand needle into the slipknot as if it were a stitch you were about to knit.

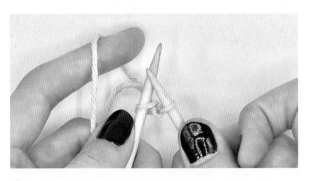

2. Wrap yarn and pull a loop through.

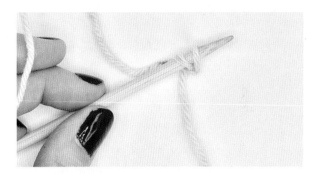

3. Place this loop onto your left-hand needle.

4. Insert the tip of your right-hand needle between the two stitches on your left-hand needle.

5. Wrap yarn and pull a loop through, as you did in Step 2.

6. Repeat Steps 4 and 5 until you have cast on the number of stitches specified in the pattern.

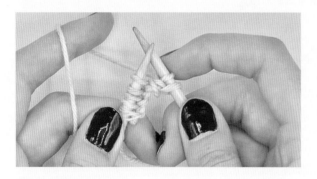

7. Knit two stitches.

8. Pass the second stitch on your right-hand needle over and off.

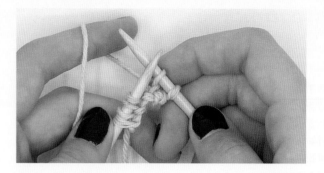

9. Knit another stitch.

10. Pass the second stitch on your right-hand needle over and off, just as you did in Step 8. You have now bound off two stitches.

Repeat steps 9 and 10 once more, for a total of three bound-off stitches.

11. Place the stitch on your right-hand needle back onto your left-hand needle.

12. Insert right-hand needle between first two stitches on left-hand needle and repeat from Step 5 until you have the correct number of stitches.

GARLIC CLOVE
HAT

Sometimes a slouchy hat is just the thing. This one features bands of easy-to-work eyelets to give it a special flair.

Materials

YARN: Toby Roxane Designs Beautilitarian DK (100% superwash merino; 250 yd./229 m per 3.5 oz./100 g)
>> Garlic Clove: 1 skein

NEEDLES:
>> Size US 5/3.75 mm circular needle, 16 in./40 cm
>> Size US 7/4.5 mm circular needle, 16 in./40 cm, and double-pointed needles (1 set)

NOTIONS: Stitch markers (5), tapestry needle

Gauge

20 sts and 28 rnds = 4 in./10 cm over stockinette stitch on larger needles

Finished Measurements

Brim: 21 in./53 cm circumference when stretched

Skills Used

>> Joining/knitting in the round
>> M1 increases
>> K2tog/ssk decreases
>> Using double-pointed needles
>> Yarn over increases

Directions

BRIM

Using smaller circular needle, CO 88 sts. Place beginning-of-rnd (BOR) marker and join to work in the round, being careful not to twist sts.

Rnd 1: [K2, p2] to end.

This rnd establishes ribbing. Repeat Rnd 1 nine more times, for a total of 10 rnds of ribbing.

BODY

Switch to larger circular needle.

Next rnd: [K3, M1] to last 4 sts, k4—116 sts.

*Knit 7 rnds.

Work lace stripe as follows:

Rnd 1: Purl.

Rnd 2: Knit.

Rnd 3: [K2tog, yo] to end.

Rnd 4: Knit.

Rnd 5: Purl.

Repeat from * twice more.

Knit 2 rnds.

CROWN

Continue as follows, switching to dpns when sts no longer fit comfortably around circular needle.

Rnd 1: K10, k2tog, knit to end—115 sts.

Rnd 2: [K23, pm] to last 23 sts, knit to end.

Rnd 3: [K2tog, knit to 2 sts before m, ssk] to end—10 sts decreased.

Rnd 4: Knit.

Rnds 5–16: Repeat previous 2 rnds 6 more times—45 sts (9 sts in each section).

Rnds 17–18: Repeat Rnd 3 twice more—25 sts (5 sts in each section).

Rnd 19: [K2tog twice, k1] to end—15 sts (3 sts in each section).

Break yarn, leaving a tail approximately 8 in./20 cm long. Thread tail through tapestry needle, run through all remaining sts, and pull tight. Weave in end on inside of hat.

Weave in any remaining ends, block if desired, and wear proudly!

FLINT CORN HAT

This super-simple hat has one small detail that makes it truly unique: the garter tab and button ruche the fabric in a terribly fetching way, making this cloche-style hat a real head turner.

Materials

YARN: Toby Roxane Designs Elegance Fingering (80% superwash merino, 10% cashmere, 10% nylon; 435 yd./398 m per 3.5 oz./100 g)
  » Flint Corn: 1 skein for Main Color
Toby Roxane Designs Chandelier Fingering (100% superwash merino; 435 yd./398 m per 3.5 oz./100 g)
  » Abigail: Approximately 25 yd./18.3 m for Contrasting Color

NEEDLES:
  » Size US 3/3.25 mm double-pointed needles; you will only need 2
  » Size US 5/3.75 mm circular needle, 16 in./40 cm, and double-pointed needles (1 set)

NOTIONS: Stitch markers (6), tapestry needle, 1 small button (approximately ½ in./13 mm)

Gauge

24 sts and 32 rnds = 4 in./10 cm in stockinette stitch

Finished Measurements

Sizes: Small (Medium, Large)
Circumference: 19 (20, 21) in./47.5 (50, 52.5) cm
Height: 9½ (10, 10½) in./24 (25, 26.5) cm (adjustable)

Skills Used

  » Joining/knitting in the round
  » K2tog/ssk decreases
  » Using double-pointed needles
  » Picking up stitches in inside of hat (See tutorial on page 64.)

Directions

Using circular needle and MC, CO 114 (120, 126) sts. Place beginning-of-rnd (BOR) marker and join to work in the round, being careful not to twist your sts.

Rnd 1: Knit.

Rnd 2: Purl.

Work in stockinette stitch (knit every rnd) until hat measures 6¼ (6¾, 7¼) in./16 (17, 18.5) cm or 3 in./8 cm less than desired finished length.

Decrease for crown as follows, switching to dpns when sts no longer fit comfortably around circular needle:

Rnd 1: [K17 (18, 19), k2tog, pm] to end—108 (114, 120) sts.

Tip: The markers you place here should be a different color or type from your BOR marker, so that you can tell them apart.

Rnds 2, 4, 6, 8, 10, 12, 14, 16, 18: Knit.

Rnds 3, 5, 7, 9, 11, 13, 15, 17, 19, 20, 21, 22, and 23: [Knit to 2 sts before m, k2tog, slm] to end—6 sts decreased each rnd; 30 (36, 42) sts remain after Rnd 23.

Rnd 24: [K2tog] to end—15 (18, 21) sts.

Sizes Small and Large ONLY:

Rnd 25: [K2tog, k1] to end—10 (-, 14) sts.

Size Medium ONLY:

Rnd 25: [K2tog] to end— - (9, -) sts.

Break yarn, leaving a tail approximately 12 in./30 cm long. Thread tail through tapestry needle, run through all remaining sts, and pull tight. Weave in end on inside of hat.

TAB

Turn the hat so that you're looking at the WS with the bottom of the hat facing up. Using the smaller dpns, pick up and knit 7 sts about 4 in./10 cm from the edge (see Step 1 below).

Knit every row until tab measures 2½ in./6.5 cm, and then work buttonhole as follows:

Buttonhole Row: K3, yo, k2tog, k2.

Knit 4 more rows.

Next row: Ssk, k3, k2tog—5 sts.

Next row: Ssk, k1, k2tog—3 sts.
BO all sts.

FINISHING

Try hat on and decide how high up from the brim you wish to sew the button. Sew button to hat to correspond to tab.

Weave in all ends, block if desired, and wear proudly!

TUTORIAL: PICKING UP STITCHES
ON INSIDE OF HAT

1. As per the pattern, choose a spot on the inside of the hat approximately 4 in./10 cm from the edge. Insert the tip of your needle under a strand.

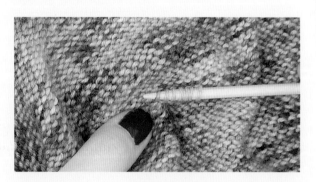

2. Making sure to stay along the same row of stitches, pick up seven stitches and place them on your needle.

3. Using your contrasting color, knit all seven stitches.

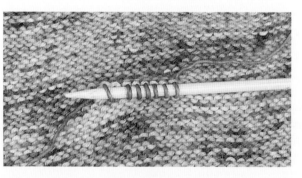

4. You are now ready to continue knitting the tab.

SCRAP BLANKET

As you finish more and more projects, you'll accumulate lots of leftover yarn. Little balls of different colors aren't always enough to make an entire project, but they're perfect for this adorable baby blanket. Gather up all your DK and light-worsted weight bits and bobs, and maybe invest in another whole skein or two to pull them all together, and voilà! The perfect baby gift! You could even make a bigger one to use as a bedspread or a cozy couch blanket.

Materials

YARN: Toby Roxane Designs Beautilitarian DK (100% superwash merino; 250 yd./229 m per 3.5 oz./100 g) in assorted colors, totaling approximately 2,000 yd./ 1,829 m.

NEEDLES: Size US 7/4.5 mm circular needle, 24 in./60 cm or 32 in./80 cm

NOTIONS: Stitch markers (8), tapestry needle

Gauge

18 sts and 34 rows = 4 in./10 cm over garter stitch, after blocking

Finished Measurements

36 in./91.5 cm square

Skills Used

» Kfb increases
» Yarn over increases
» K2tog/ssk decreases
» Picking up stitches along a garter stitch edge (See tutorial on page 69.)
» K2tog tbl (through back loop)

Directions

Note: Instructions will not signify when to change colors—it's up to you!
CO 2 sts.

SETUP SECTION

Row 1 (RS): Kfb twice—4 sts.
Row 2 (WS): Knit.
Row 3: K1, kfb twice, k1—6 sts.
Row 4: Knit.

INCREASE SECTION

Row 1 (RS): K2, yo, knit to last 2 sts, yo, k2—2 sts increased.
Row 2 (WS): Knit.

Repeat Rows 1 and 2 of Increase Section until work measures 15 in./38 cm **along side edge** (not from the point of the triangle straight up to the needle—see diagram on page 68), ending with a WS row.

DECREASE SECTION

Row 1 (RS): K2, yo, ssk twice, knit to last 6 sts, k2tog twice, yo, k2—2 sts decreased.
Row 2 (WS): Knit.

Repeat Rows 1 and 2 of Decrease Section until 12 sts remain, ending with a WS row.

FINAL CORNER

Row 1 (RS): K2, yo, ssk twice, k2tog twice, yo, k2—10 sts.
Row 2 (and all following WS rows): Knit.

pick up 1 st for corner. Repeat from * twice more (three sides completed), and then pm, pick up sts along remaining side until you reach the starting point, and pm for the beginning of rnd. You should now have sts picked up around all 4 sides of the blanket, with a single corner st isolated by markers at each corner (see diagram below). Do not turn work to WS; you will now work in the round to complete the Border.

Rnd 1: [K1, slm, yo, knit to m, yo, slm] four times.
Rnd 2: Knit.

Repeat Rnds 1 and 2 until border measures 3 in./8 cm.

Using a needle at least 2 sizes larger, BO all sts **loosely** as follows: *K2tog tbl, slip st from right-hand needle back to left-hand needle. Repeat from * until 1 st remains. Break yarn and pull through.

Note:

It's nearly always a good idea to bind off loosely, but when a pattern suggests that you use a larger needle *and* makes a point of telling you to bind off **loosely**, the designer really means it! In this case, the reason is that garter stitch fabric is especially stretchy. When you block this blanket, it will grow a bit bigger, and it's important to bind off loosely enough to ensure that the bind-off is sufficiently flexible to stretch with the rest of the blanket.

Row 3: K3, ssk, k2tog, k3—8 sts.
Row 5: K2, ssk, k2tog, k2—6 sts.
Row 7: K1, ssk, k2tog, k1—4 sts.
Row 9: Ssk, k2tog—2 sts.
Pass the first st over the second and off the needle—1 st remains. DO NOT break yarn.

BORDER

With RS facing and 1 st on needle, *pm, pick up 1 st for every two rows along side edge of blanket (see photo tutorial on page 69) until 1 st before the corner, pm,

Weave in ends, block, and wrap up a baby!

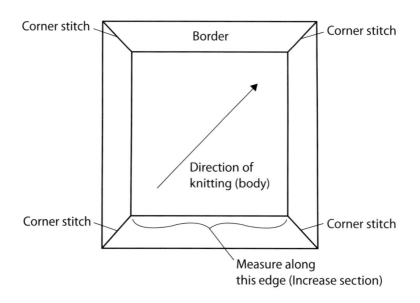

Corner stitch — Border — Corner stitch

Direction of knitting (body)

Corner stitch — Corner stitch

Measure along this edge (Increase section)

TUTORIAL: PICKING UP STITCHES ALONG A GARTER STITCH EDGE

1. Turn your work so that the Right Side is facing you. Notice the "bumps" along the edge of your work. In between each of these bumps is a strand. Each bump represents one row, and each strand represents one row. (When instructed to "pick up 1 st for every two rows along side edge," it means you should pick up a stitch in each strand, skipping the bumps.) Insert your needle under the first strand at the corner of your work.

2. Wrap the yarn around the needle and pull through. This is your first picked up stitch.

3. Insert your needle under the next strand.

4. Wrap the yarn around the needle and pull through, just as you did in Step 2.

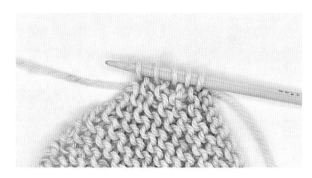

5. Repeat until you have picked up the appropriate number of stitches.

PSYCHIC RAINBOW MITTENS

Every knitter should have a good, basic mitten pattern in their repertoire. Pro tip: Make one to pair with my Beer Mitt pattern (bit.ly/beermitt).

Materials

YARN: Toby Roxane Designs Velvet Chunky (100% superwash merino; 109 yd./100 m per 3.5 oz./100 g)
» Psychic Rainbow: 1 skein
NEEDLES:
» Size US 8/5 mm double-pointed needles (1 set)
» Size US 10/6 mm double-pointed needles (1 set)
NOTIONS: Locking marker (optional), stitch marker (1), scrap yarn, tapestry needle

Gauge

14 sts and 20 rnds = 4 in./10 cm over stockinette stitch

Finished Measurements

8 in./20 cm hand circumference

Skills Used

» Joining/working in the round
» M1R/M1L increases
» Transferring stitches to and from waste yarn
» Picking up stitches
» K2tog/ssk decreases
» Using double-pointed needles
» Backward loop cast-on

Directions (Make 2)

Using smaller dpns, CO 28 sts. Being careful not to twist your sts, join to work in the round.

Tip:

When you're knitting on double-pointed needles, you don't need to place a stitch marker for the beginning of the round, since it is usually between two needles. I recommend hanging a locking stitch marker from the first stitch of the round to remind you where it is. Move the marker up toward the needles periodically so it remains easily visible.

Ribbing Rnd: [K1, p1] to end.

Repeat Ribbing Rnd 9 more times, for a total of 10 rnds of ribbing.

Switch to larger dpns.

Knit 10 rnds.

Work thumb gusset:

Rnd 1: M1R, k1, M1L, pm, knit to end—30 sts.

Rnd 2: Knit.

Rnd 3: M1R, knit to m, M1L, slm, knit to end—2 sts increased.

Repeat previous 2 rnds twice more until you have a total of 9 sts before marker—36 sts total.

Work Rnd 2 once more.

Next rnd: Slip 9 thumb sts onto scrap yarn, remove m, using backward loop method CO 1 st, knit to end—28 sts.

Knit until mitten measures 5 in./13 cm from top of ribbing (or 1½ in./4 cm shorter than the tip of your longest finger).

Decrease as follows:

Rnd 1: Ssk, k10, k2tog, pm, ssk, knit to last 2 sts, k2tog—24 sts.

Rnd 2: Knit.

Rnd 3: Ssk, knit to 2 sts before m, k2tog, slm, ssk, knit to last 2 sts, k2tog—4 sts decreased.

Repeat previous 2 rnds twice more until 12 sts remain.

Next rnd: [K2tog] around, removing m when you come to it—6 sts.

Break yarn, leaving a 10 in./25 cm tail. Thread tail through tapestry needle, run through all remaining sts, and pull tight. Weave in end on inside.

THUMB

Distribute 9 held thumb sts onto larger dpns. Pick up 1 st in the gap between thumb and hand—10 sts.

Knit all rnds until thumb measures 1¾ in./4.5 cm (or ¼ in./0.5 cm shorter than the length of your thumb).

Next rnd: [K2tog] around—5 sts.

Break yarn, leaving a 6 in./15 cm tail. Thread tail through tapestry needle, run through all remaining sts, and pull tight. Weave in end on inside.

Weave in the end between the thumb and the hand on the inside, using it to close any gaps.

Weave in any remaining ends and wear proudly!

TREEHOUSE SOCKS

This is a pattern for a very basic pair of socks ("vanilla socks," as many seasoned knitters call them). This one is a little different, though. Take your shoes off and have a look at your feet. Is one of your middle toes longer than the rest? If so, great! Most standard sock patterns will fit your foot, and you should use the Symmetrical Toe option in this pattern. Is your big toe the longest? Mine, too! I've found that the way most sock patterns are written don't fit my feet well, so I've included an Asymmetrical Toe option in this pattern (the pair shown in the photos use this toe option). Note that the right and left socks will be slightly different if you use this toe option.

Materials

YARN: Toby Roxane Designs Contact Sport (100% superwash merino; 328 yd./300 m per 3.5 oz./100 g)
   » Treehouse: 1 skein
NEEDLES: Size US 2/2.75 mm double-pointed needles (or needles for your preferred method of working small circumferences in the round)
NOTIONS: Stitch markers (3), tapestry needle

Gauge

30 sts and 41 rnds = 4 in./10 cm over stockinette stitch

Finished Measurements

To fit ankle/foot circumference 8 (8½, 9) in./20.5 (21.5, 23) cm. Cuff and foot length can be adjusted as desired, but keep in mind that if you wish to make the cuff significantly longer than 6 in./15 cm, and/or the foot significantly longer than 9 in./23 cm, you may need an extra skein of yarn.

Skills Used

   » Joining/knitting in the round
   » K2tog/ssk decreases
   » Picking up stitches along a garter stitch edge (See tutorial on page 69.)
   » Grafting

Pattern Note

When instructed to slip a stitch, it should be slipped purlwise with yarn in back unless otherwise noted.

Tip:

When knitting socks from the top down, it's a good idea to cast on very loosely, so that the top of the sock will stretch enough to fit over your heel when you're putting it on. You might even want to cast your stitches onto a needle a size or two larger than your gauge needle (the needle size that gives you the gauge listed) and then switch to the gauge needle for the first round.

Directions

LEG

CO 50 (54, 58) sts. Place beginning-of-round (BOR) m and join to work in the round, being careful not to twist sts. Knit every rnd until sock measures 6 in./15 cm (or desired length).

HEEL FLAP

Note: Heel flap is worked back and forth in rows across only the first 25 (27, 29) sts of the round.

Row 1 (RS): [Sl1, k1] to last st, k1.
Row 2 (WS): Sl1, purl to end.
Repeat Rows 1 and 2 until heel flap measures 2 in./5 cm.

TURN HEEL

Row 1 (RS): Sl1, k14, ssk, k1, turn.
Row 2 (WS): Sl1, p6, p2tog, p1, turn.
Row 3: Sl1, knit to 1 st before gap, ssk, k1, turn.
Row 4: Sl1, purl to 1 st before gap, p2tog, p1, turn.
Repeat Rows 3 and 4 until 1 st remains at each end.
Next row (RS): Sl1, knit to 1 st before gap, ssk.
Next row (WS): Sl1, purl to 1 st before gap, p2tog.

Setup gusset (RS): Sl1, knit to end. Pick up and knit 1 st for every slipped st along side of heel flap, pick up and knit 1 st in the gap between heel flap and instep, pmA, knit across live sts, pmB, pick up and knit 1 st for every slipped st along remaining side of heel flap.

GUSSET

Place beginning-of-round (BOR) marker; you will now begin working in the round again.
Rnd 1: Knit to 2 sts before mA, k2tog, slm, knit to mB, slm, ssk, knit to end—2 sts decreased.
Rnd 2: Knit.
Rnd 3: Knit to 2 sts before mA, k2tog, slm, knit to mB, slm, ssk, knit to end—2 sts decreased.
Repeat Rnds 2 and 3 until 50 (54, 58) sts remain.
Remove BORm and knit to mB, removing mA. This is your new BORm.

FOOT

Work even (knit every rnd) until foot measures 2 in./5 cm shorter than the tip of your longest toe. Choose whether you will work the Symmetrical or Asymmetrical Toe and continue with the style chosen.

SYMMETRICAL TOE (Use this toe option if your middle toe is the longest.)

Rnd 1: K25 (27, 29) sts, pm, knit to end.
Rnd 2: K1, ssk, knit to 3 sts before m, k2tog, k1, slm, k1, ssk, knit to 3 sts before end, k2tog, k1—4 sts decreased.
Rnd 3: Knit.
Repeat Rnds 2 and 3 until you have a total of 22 (22, 26) sts remaining. Divide sts evenly between two needles and graft together (see tutorial on page 77).

ASYMMETRICAL TOE (Use this toe option if your big toe is the longest.)

RIGHT SOCK

Rnd 1: K25 (27, 29) sts, pm, knit to end.
Rnd 2: K1, ssk, knit to last 3 sts, k2tog, k1—2 sts decreased.
Repeat Rnd 2 nine more times—30 (34, 38) sts.
Rnd 3: K1, ssk, knit to 3 sts before m, k2tog, k1, slm, k1, ssk, knit to 3 sts before end, k2tog, k1—4 sts decreased.
Rnd 4: As Rnd 2.

Repeat Rnds 3 and 4 twice more—12 (16, 20) sts. Divide remaining sts evenly between two needles and graft together (see tutorial).

LEFT SOCK
Rnd 1: K25 (27, 29) sts, pm, knit to end.
Rnd 2: Knit to 3 sts before m, k2tog, k1, slm, k1, ssk, knit to end—2 sts decreased.
Repeat Rnd 2 nine more times—30 (34, 38) sts.

Rnd 3: K1, ssk, knit to 3 sts before m, k2tog, k1, slm, k1, ssk, knit to 3 sts before end, k2tog, k1—4 sts decreased.
Rnd 4: As Rnd 2.
Repeat Rnds 3 and 4 twice more—12 (16, 20) sts. Divide remaining sts evenly between two needles and graft together (see tutorial).

Weave in ends, block if desired, and wear proudly!

TUTORIAL: GRAFTING

1. Start by making sure you have the same number of stitches on both needles. Break yarn, leaving a tail approximately 12 in./30 cm long. Thread the tail through a tapestry needle.

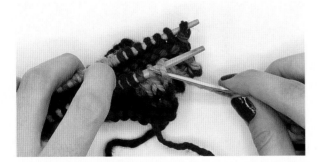

2. Insert the tapestry needle through the first stitch on your front needle as if to purl.

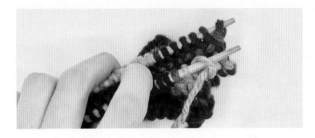

3. Pull yarn through.

4. Insert the tapestry needle through the first stitch on your back needle as if to knit, and pull through.

5. Insert the tapestry needle through the first stitch on your front needle again, this time as if to knit.

6. Slip this stitch off the needle and pull the yarn through.

9. Slip this stitch off the needle and pull the yarn through, as you did in Step 6.

7. Insert the tapestry needle through the next stitch on your front needle as if to purl. Pull yarn through (do not slip this stitch off the needle).

10. Insert the tapestry needle through the next stitch on your back needle as if to knit. Pull yarn through (do not slip this stitch off the needle).

8. Insert the tapestry needle through the first stitch on your back needle as if to purl.

Repeat Steps 5–10, ending with Steps 5–7, slipping the last stitch off the last needle.

A POINTY RECKONING PULLOVER

Ready to make a sweater? With its simple, stockinette stitch body accented by a few contrasting garter stripes and easy round yoke construction method, this is the perfect first-sweater project.

Materials

YARN: Toby Roxane Designs Velvet Chunky (100% superwash merino; 109 yd./100 m per 3.5 oz./100 g)
  - » A Pointy Reckoning: 5 (5, 5, 6, 6, 6, 7) skeins for Main Color
  - » Abigail: 1 skein for Contrasting Color

NEEDLES: Size US 10½/6.5 mm circular needles, 16 in./40 cm and 24 in./60 cm (or longer), and double-pointed needles (1 set)

NOTIONS: Stitch markers (3), waste yarn, tapestry needle

Gauge

13 sts and 18 rnds = 4 in./10 cm over stockinette stitch, after blocking

Sizes

XSmall (Small, Medium, Large, XLarge, XXLarge, XXXLarge) To fit bust sizes 30 (34, 38, 42, 46, 50, 54) in./76 (86, 96.5, 106.5, 117, 127, 137) cm. See schematic for finished measurements. Sweater is intended to fit with approximately 4–5 in./9–13 cm of positive ease.

Skills Used

  - » Joining/working in the round
  - » M1 increases
  - » Short rows; wrap and turn (See tutorial on page 84.)
  - » Cable cast-on
  - » K2tog/ssk decreases
  - » Picking up stitches from waste yarn
  - » Picking up and knitting from bound off stitches

Directions

Using CC and shorter circular needle, CO 78 (82, 82, 86, 86, 88, 88) sts.

Switch to MC and knit one row. Being careful not to twist sts, place beginning-of-rnd (BOR) marker and join to work in the round.

Size XSmall ONLY:
Increase Rnd 1: K1, [M1, k3] to last 2 sts, M1, k2—104 sts.

Sizes Small, Medium, and Large ONLY:
Increase Rnd 1: K1, [M1, k3] - (7, 5, 3, -, -, -) times, [M1, k2] - (19, 25, 33, -, -, -) times, [M1, k3] - (7, 5, 3, -, -, -) times, M1, k1— - (116, 118, 126, -, -, -) sts.

Sizes XLarge, XXLarge, and XXXLarge ONLY:
Increase Rnd 1: K1, [M1, k1] - (-, -, -, 3, 6, 14) times, [M1, k2] - (-, -, -, 39, 37, 29) times, [M1, k1] - (-, -, -, 3, 6, 14) times, M1, k1— - (-, -, -, 132, 138, 146) sts.

All Sizes:
Next rnd (setup for short rows): K42 (46, 47, 50, 53, 55, 58), pmA, k20 (24, 24, 26, 26, 28, 30), pmB, knit to end.

Work short rows as follows:
Row 1 (RS): Knit to 1 st before mA, w&t.
Row 2 (WS): Purl to 1 st before mB, w&t.
Row 3 (RS): Knit to 5 sts before wrapped st, w&t.
Row 4 (WS): Purl to 5 sts before wrapped st, w&t.
Repeat Rows 3 and 4 until you have a total of 6 (6, 6, 7, 7, 8) wrapped sts on each side.
Next row (RS): Knit to BORm, hiding wraps and removing mA and mB as you go.

You will now resume working in the round.
Next rnd: Knit, hiding remaining wraps as you go.
Knit 1 more rnd.

Size XSmall ONLY:
Increase Rnd 2: K2, [M1, k5] to last 2 sts, M1, k2—125 sts.

Size Small ONLY:
Increase Rnd 2: K2, [M1, k5] 4 times, [M1, k4] 18 times, [M1, k5] 4 times, M1, k2—143 sts.

Sizes Medium to XXXLarge ONLY:
Increase Rnd 2: K2, [M1, k3] - (-, 1, 3, 10, 13, 21) time(s), [M1, k4] - (-, 27, 26, 17, 14, 4) times, [M1, k3] - (-, 1, 3, 10, 13, 21) time(s), M1, k2— - (-, 148, 159, 170, 179, 193) sts.

All Sizes:
Knit 7 (9, 10, 11, 13, 14, 15) rnds.

Size XSmall ONLY:
Increase Rnd 3: K2, [M1, k6] to last 3 sts, M1, k3—146 sts.

Size Small ONLY:
Increase Rnd 3: K2, [M1, k6] 4 times, [M1, k5] 18 times, [M1, k6] 4 times, M1, k3—170 sts.

Sizes Medium and XLarge ONLY:
Increase Rnd 3: K2, [M1, k5] - (-, 14, -, 9, -, -) times, [M1, k4] - (-, 1, -, 19, -, -) time(s), [M1, k5] - (-, 14, -, 9, -, -) times, M1, k2— - (-, 178, -, 208, -, -) sts.

Sizes Large, XXLarge, and XXXLarge ONLY:
Increase Rnd 3: K2, [M1, k4] - (-, -, 3, -, 13, 21) times, [M1, k5] - (-, -, 26, -, 14, 4) times, [M1, k4] - (-, -, 3, -, 13, 21) times, M1, k3— - (-, -, 192, -, 220, 240) sts.

All Sizes:
Knit 4 rnds.

Switch to CC and work 4 rnds as follows:
Rnds 1 and 3: Knit.
Rnds 2 and 4: Purl.

Switch to MC and knit 3 (3, 4, 5, 6, 7, 8) rnds.

Size XSmall ONLY:
Increase Rnd 4: K4, [M1, k9] 5 times, [M1, k8] 6 times, [M1, k9] 5 times, M1, k4—163 sts.

Sizes Small, Medium, and Large ONLY:
Increase Rnd 4: K4, [M1, k7] - (3, 7, 8, -, -, -) times, [M1, k8] - (15, 9, 9, -, -, -) times, [M1, k7] - (3, 7, 8, -, -, -) times, M1, k4— - (192, 202, 218, -, -, -) sts.

Sizes XLarge, XXLarge, and XXXLarge ONLY:
Increase Rnd 4: K3, [M1, k7] - (-, -, -, 14, 11, 6) times, [M1, k6] - (-, -, -, 1, 10, 25) time(s), [M1, k7] - (-, -, -, 14, 11, 6) times, M1, k3— - (-, -, -, 238, 253, 278) sts.

All Sizes:
Knit 1 rnd.

Divide for sleeves as follows:
Remove BORm. Slip 32 (39, 40, 43, 45, 48, 52) sleeve sts to waste yarn, turn work and cable CO 7 (7, 9, 9, 9, 10, 10) sts, k50 (57, 61, 66, 74, 79, 87), slip 32 (39, 40, 43, 45, 48, 52) sleeve sts to waste yarn, turn work and cable CO 7 (7, 9, 9, 9, 10, 10) sts, knit to end—113 (128, 140, 150, 166, 177, 194) sts.

BODY
Work even (knit every rnd) until body measures 13 in./33 cm (or desired length) from underarm.
Next rnd: Purl.
Switch to CC.
BO all sts.

SLEEVES
Transfer held sts for one sleeve from waste yarn to dpns. Rejoin MC and, starting at center of underarm, pick up and knit 4 (4, 5, 5, 5, 5, 5) sts, knit across all live sts, pick up and knit 3 (3, 4, 4, 4, 5, 5) sts from remaining underarm CO sts—39 (46, 49, 52, 54, 58, 62) sts. Pm and join to work in the round.
Knit 13 (9, 9, 8, 15, 11, 18) rnds.
Next rnd (Decrease Rnd): K1, k2tog, knit to last 3 sts, ssk, k1—2 sts decreased.
*Knit 9 (5, 5, 4, 3, 3, 2) rnds.
Work Decrease Rnd.
Repeat from * until you have 27 (26, 29, 28, 28, 30, 30) sts remaining.
Work even (knit all rnds) until sleeve measures 14¼ in./35.5 cm (or desired length) from underarm.
Next rnd: Purl.
Switch to CC.
BO all sts.

Weave in ends, block, and wear proudly!

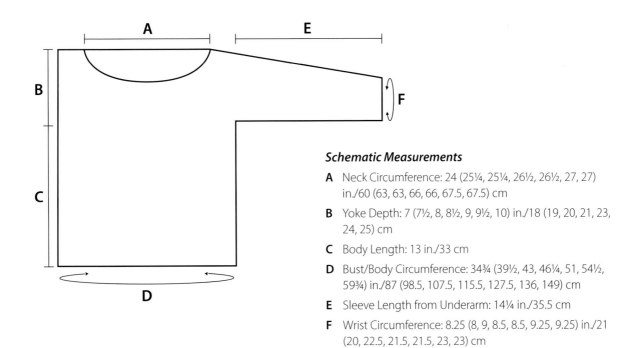

Schematic Measurements

A Neck Circumference: 24 (25¼, 25¼, 26½, 26½, 27, 27) in./60 (63, 63, 66, 66, 67.5, 67.5) cm

B Yoke Depth: 7 (7½, 8, 8½, 9, 9½, 10) in./18 (19, 20, 21, 23, 24, 25) cm

C Body Length: 13 in./33 cm

D Bust/Body Circumference: 34¾ (39½, 43, 46¼, 51, 54½, 59¾) in./87 (98.5, 107.5, 115.5, 127.5, 136, 149) cm

E Sleeve Length from Underarm: 14¼ in./35.5 cm

F Wrist Circumference: 8.25 (8, 9, 8.5, 8.5, 9.25, 9.25) in./21 (20, 22.5, 21.5, 21.5, 23, 23) cm

TUTORIAL: SHORT ROWS

Short rows are used to add more fabric to one area of your knitting. For the Pointy Reckoning Pullover, short rows are used to raise the back neckline a little higher than the front neckline. In the Enchanted Wood Cardigan (see page 91), they are used to add more fabric to the upper part of the shawl collar.

ON RIGHT SIDE OF WORK

1. When you reach the point where you are instructed to wrap and turn (w&t), slip the next stitch purlwise onto your right-hand needle without knitting it.

2. Bring the working yarn to the front of your work.

3. Move the slipped stitch back to your left-hand needle. You have now wrapped the yarn around this stitch.

4. Turn your work over to the wrong side and bring the working yarn to the front. Continue with the pattern directions.

ON WRONG SIDE OF WORK

If you need to do a wrap and turn on the wrong side (the purl side) of your work, work the following steps:

1. When you reach the point where you are instructed to wrap and turn, bring the working yarn to the back of your work.

2. Slip the next stitch purlwise onto your right-hand needle without working it.

3. Bring the working yarn to the front of your work again.

4. Move your slipped stitch back onto your left-hand needle. Turn your work over and continue with the pattern directions.

— — — — — — — — —

After working a section of short rows, you will have several wrapped stitches. In garter stitch, there is no need to hide the wraps—the "bars" are disguised within the ridges of the stitch pattern. However, when they appear in stockinette stitch, many people prefer to hide them by knitting them together with the stitch they wrap. When instructed to "knit, hiding wraps as you go," work the following steps when you come to a wrapped stitch:

1. The wrap will look like a bar across the bottom of the stitch on the needle. Insert your right-hand needle underneath this bar.

2. Insert your needle into the stitch, as if to knit.

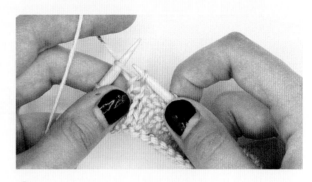

3. Draw the yarn through both the stitch and the wrap. The wrap will come off your needle. Slide the stitch off your needle as usual.

You have now knit the wrap together with the stitch. Continue with the pattern directions.

BLUEBIRD
CARDIGAN

Here we have a lovely, simple cardigan. Knit in stockinette stitch with a wide garter stitch hem and cuffs, it will quickly become a wardrobe staple.

Materials

YARN: Toby Roxane Designs Polwarth DK (100% superwash Polwarth wool; 252 yd./230 m per 3.5 oz./ 100 g)

» Bluebird: 4 (4, 5, 5, 5, 5, 6) skeins

NEEDLES:

» Size US 6/4 mm circular needle, 24 in./60 cm or longer

» Size US 7/4.5 mm circular needle, 24 in./60 cm or longer, and double-pointed needles (1 set)

NOTIONS: Stitch markers (8), 7 small buttons (⅝ in./ 15 mm)

Gauge

21 sts and 29 rows = 4 in./10 cm over stockinette stitch on larger needles, after blocking

Sizes

XSmall (Small, Medium, Large, XLarge, XXLarge, XXXLarge) To fit bust sizes 30 (34, 38, 42, 46, 50, 54) in./76 (86, 96.5, 106.5, 117, 127, 137) cm. Sweater is intended to fit with 2–4 in./5–10 cm of positive ease. See schematic for finished measurements.

Skills Used

» Yarn over increases

» Transferring stitches to and from waste yarn

» Picking up stitches along a stockinette stitch edge (See tutorial on page 96.)

» Cable cast-on

» K2tog/ssk decreases

Pattern Notes

When instructed to work Increase Row, work as follows:

» **If RS row:** [Knit to m, yo, slm, k1, slm, yo] four times, knit to end—8 sts increased.

» **If WS row:** [Purl to m, yo, slm, p1, slm, yo] four times, purl to end—8 sts increased.

When instructed to work even, knit all sts on RS rows and purl all sts on WS rows (do not work any increases or decreases).

Directions

Using larger circular needle, CO 140 (128, 130, 126, 118, 116, 128) sts.

Setup row (RS): K24 (24, 25, 25, 26, 27, 28) for left front, pm, k1, pm, k20 (14, 13, 11, 5, 2, 6) for left sleeve, pm, k1, pm, k48 (48, 50, 50, 52, 54, 56) for back, pm, k1, pm, k20 (14, 13, 11, 5, 2, 6) for right sleeve, pm, k1, pm, knit to end for right front.

Purl 1 row.

Begin raglan increases as follows:

*Work Increase Row. (See "Pattern Notes" above.)

Work even for 3 (2, 2, 1, 1, 1, 1) row(s).

Repeat from * 3 (4, 4, 5, 6, 7, 7) more times—28 (29, 30, 31, 33, 35, 36) sts each front; 28 (24, 23, 23, 19, 18, 22) sts each sleeve; 56 (58, 60, 62, 66, 70, 72) back sts; 172 (168, 170, 174, 174, 180, 192) sts total.

**Work Increase Row.

Work even for 4 (3, 2, 2, 2, 2, 2) rows.

Repeat from ** 4 (7, 9, 12, 13, 14, 16) more times—33 (37, 40, 44, 47, 50, 53) sts each front; 38 (40, 43, 49, 47, 48, 56) sts each sleeve; 66 (74, 80, 88, 94, 100, 106) back sts; 212 (232, 250, 278, 286, 300, 328) sts total.

***Work Increase Row.

Work even for 3 (2, 2, 1, 1, 1, 1) row(s).

Repeat from *** 3 (3, 4, 4, 5, 6, 7) more times—37 (41, 45, 49, 53, 57, 61) sts each front; 46 (48, 53, 59, 59, 62, 72) sts each sleeve; 74 (82, 90, 98, 106, 114, 122) back sts; 244 (264, 290, 318, 334, 356, 392) sts total.

Divide body and sleeves:

If RS is not facing for next row, purl 1 row.

Next row (RS): *Knit to m, remove m, slip 1 st onto waste yarn, remove m, slip 46 (48, 53, 59, 59, 62, 72) sleeve sts onto waste yarn, remove m, slip 1 st onto waste yarn, remove m, turn work and cable CO 10 (14, 15, 18, 21, 24, 26) sts, turn work; repeat from * once more then knit to end—168 (192, 210, 232, 254, 276, 296) sts.

BODY

Work even until cardigan measures 12 in./30.5 cm from underarm or 2 in./5 cm less than total desired length. Work in garter stitch (knit all rows) for 2 in./5 cm more. BO all sts.

SLEEVES

Transfer held sts for one sleeve onto dpns. Rejoin yarn and, starting at center of underarm, pick up and knit 5 (7, 7, 9, 10, 12, 13) sts, knit across all live sts, pick up and knit

5 (7, 8, 9, 11, 12, 13) sts from remaining underarm CO sts. Pm and join to work in the round—58 (64, 70, 79, 82, 88, 100) sts.

Work 13 (7, 12, 17, 13, 1, 13) rnd(s) even.

Decrease Rnd: K2, k2tog, knit to last 4 sts, ssk, k2—2 sts decreased.

Work in stockinette stitch (knit all rnds) and repeat Decrease Rnd every 6 (6, 5, 4, 4, 4, 3) rnds 14 (15, 17, 20, 21, 24, 28) more times—28 (32, 34, 37, 38, 38, 42) sts.

Work in garter stitch (knit 1 rnd, purl 1 rnd) for 1½ in./4 cm.

BO all sts.

Repeat for other sleeve.

NECKBAND

Using smaller circular needle with RS facing, pick up and knit 140 (128, 130, 126, 118, 116, 128) sts along neck edge.

Knit 4 rows.

BO all sts.

RIGHT BUTTONHOLE BAND

Using smaller circular needle with RS facing and starting at bottom right front, pick up and knit 11 sts along edge of garter stitch border, and then pick up and knit 102 (102, 110, 103, 109, 113, 118) sts along remainder of center front edge up to the top—113 (113, 121, 114, 120, 124, 129) sts.

Knit 3 rows.

Next row (RS): K5 (5, 6, 6, 5, 2, 0), *k13 (13, 14, 13, 14, 15, 16), k2tog, yo; repeat from * 6 more times, k3.

Knit 2 rows.

BO all sts.

LEFT BUTTONBAND

Using smaller circular needle with RS facing and starting at top left front, pick up and knit 102 (102, 110, 103, 109, 113, 118) sts along center front edge down to the garter border, and then pick up and knit 11 sts along edge of garter stitch border—113 (113, 121, 114, 120, 124, 129) sts.

Knit 6 rows.

BO all sts.

Weave in ends, block, sew buttons to left front opposite the buttonholes, and wear proudly!

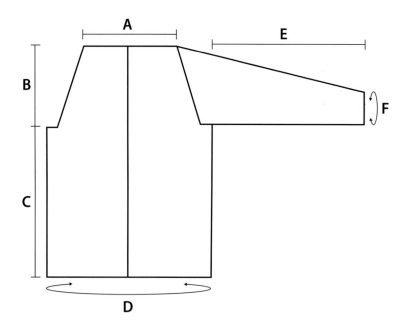

Schematic Measurements

A Back Neck Width: 9¼ (9¼, 9½, 9½, 10, 10¼, 10¾) in./23 (23, 24, 24, 25, 25.5, 26.5) cm

B Armhole Depth: 8 (8½, 8½, 8¾, 9¾, 10¾, 11¾) in./20 (20.5, 20.5, 21.5, 23.5, 26, 29) cm

C Body Length: 14 in./35.5 cm

D Bust/Body Circumference: 33 (37½, 41, 45¼, 49½, 53½, 57½) in./82.5 (94, 102.5, 113, 123.5, 134, 143.5) cm

E Sleeve Length from Underarm: 15 in./38 cm

F Wrist Circumference: 5¼ (6, 6½, 7, 7¼, 7¼, 8) in./13.5 (15, 16, 17.5, 18, 18, 20) cm

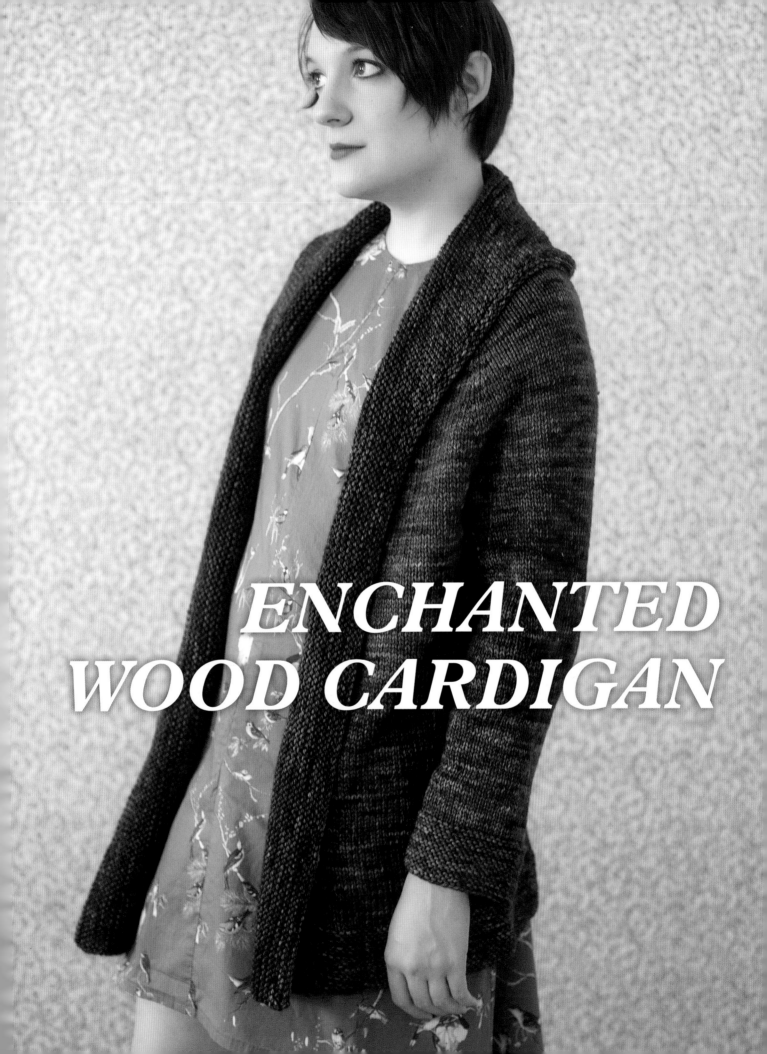

ENCHANTED
WOOD CARDIGAN

The Enchanted Wood Cardigan is slightly oversized and slouchy, with a wide shawl collar. It looks just as good over jeans as it does over a dress.

Materials

YARN: Toby Roxane Designs Velvet Aran (100% superwash merino; 181 yd./166 m per 3.5 oz./100 g)

  » Enchanted Wood: 6 (6, 7, 7, 8, 8, 9) skeins

NEEDLES: Size US 8/5 mm circular needle, 24 in./60 cm or longer, and double-pointed needles (1 set)

NOTIONS: Stitch markers (4), locking markers (2), tapestry needle

Gauge

18 sts and 26 rows = 4 in./10 cm over stockinette stitch, after blocking

Sizes

XSmall (Small, Medium, Large, XLarge, XXLarge, XXXLarge) To fit bust sizes 30 (34, 38, 42, 46, 50, 54) in./76 (86, 96.5, 106.5, 117, 127, 137) cm. Sweater is intended to fit with approximately 1–2 in./2.5–5 cm of positive ease across back. See schematic for finished measurements.

Skills Used

  » M1L/M1R increases
  » M1Lp/M1Rp increases
  » Cable cast-on
  » K2tog/ssk decreases
  » Picking up stitches from waste yarn
  » Picking up stitches along stockinette edge
  » Short rows; wrap and turn (See tutorial on page 84.)

Pattern Notes

When instructed to work Increase Row, work as follows:

» **(RS):** K1, M1R, [knit to 1 st before m, M1L, k1, slm, k1, M1R] four times, knit to last st, M1L, k1—10 sts increased.

When instructed to work even, knit all sts on RS rows and purl all sts on WS rows (do not work any increases or decreases).

Directions

Using circular needle, CO 64 (72, 66, 60, 60, 58, 64) sts.

Setup row (RS): K2, pm, k12 (14, 10, 6, 6, 4, 6), pm, k36 (40, 42, 44, 44, 46, 48), pm, k12 (14, 10, 6, 6, 4, 6), pm, k2.

*Purl 1 row.

Work Increase Row. (See "Pattern Notes" above.)

Repeat from * 2 (3, 5, 7, 8, 9, 10) more times—8 (10, 14, 18, 20, 22, 24) sts each front; 18 (22, 22, 22, 24, 24, 28) sts each sleeve; 42 (48, 54, 60, 62, 66, 70) back sts; 94 (112, 126, 140, 150, 158, 174) sts total.

**Work even for 3 rows.

Work Increase Row.

Repeat from ** 8 (8, 7, 6, 6, 7, 6) more times—26 (28, 30, 32, 34, 38, 38) sts each front; 36 (40, 38, 36, 38, 40, 42) sts each sleeve; 60 (66, 70, 74, 76, 82, 84) back sts; 184 (202, 206, 210, 220, 238, 244) sts total.

***Purl 1 row.

Work Increase Row.

Repeat from *** 2 (2, 4, 6, 7, 8, 10) more times—32 (34, 40, 46, 50, 56, 60) sts each front; 42 (46, 48, 50, 54, 58, 64) sts each sleeve; 66 (72, 80, 88, 92, 100, 106) back sts; 214 (232, 256, 280, 300, 328, 354) sts total.

Purl 1 WS row.

Divide body and sleeves as follows:

Next row (RS): K1, *knit to m, remove m, slip 42 (46, 48, 50, 55, 58, 65) sleeve sts onto waste yarn, turn work and cable CO 6 (7, 8, 10, 11, 11, 13) sts, pm, cable CO 6 (7, 8, 10, 11, 11, 13) sts, remove m; repeat from * once more, knit to end—38 (41, 48, 56, 61, 67, 73) sts each front; 78 (86, 96, 108, 114, 122, 132) back sts; 154 (168, 192, 220, 236, 256, 278) sts total. Hang a locking st marker from the first and last st on this row.

BODY

Work even in stockinette stitch until work measures 15 in./38 cm from underarm (or 4 in./10 cm shorter than desired finished length).

GARTER EDGE

Knit all rows until Garter Edge measures 4 in./10 cm.
BO all sts.

SLEEVES

Transfer held sts for one sleeve onto dpns. Rejoin yarn and, starting at center of underarm, pick up and knit 6 (7, 8,

10, 11, 11, 13) sts, knit across all live sts, pick up and knit 6 (7, 8, 10, 11, 11, 13) sts from remaining underarm CO sts. Pm and join to work in the round—54 (60, 64, 70, 76, 80, 90) sts.

Work even (knit every rnd) for 7 (5, 12, 2, 5, 5, 11) rnd(s).

Decrease Rnd: K1, k2tog, knit to last 3 sts, ssk, k1—2 sts decreased.

Continue knitting all sts and repeat Decrease Rnd every 7th (6th, 5th, 5th, 4th, 4th, 3rd) rnd 10 (12, 13, 15, 18, 18, 22) more times—32 (34, 36, 38, 38, 42, 44) sts.

Work Garter Edge as follows:

Rnd 1: Purl.

Rnd 2: Knit.

Repeat Rnds 1 and 2 until Garter Edge measures 3 in./ 7.5 cm.

BO all sts.

Repeat for other sleeve.

Note:

> When instructed to pick up stitches along a stockinette stitch edge, as for the Front Band, a pattern will often tell you to pick up and knit 2 stitches for every 3 rows. This is because knitted stitches aren't square—they're a little wider than they are tall. If you picked up stitches at a rate of 1 stitch to 1 row, your Front Band wouldn't lie flat.

FRONT BAND

Using circular needle and starting at bottom right front corner with RS facing, pick up and knit 1 st for every 2 rows along Garter Edge, and then pick up and knit 2 sts for every 3 rows along front edge. When you reach the locking stitch marker, pm on needle. Continue to pick up and knit 2 sts for every 3 rows to beginning of back neck, and then pick up and knit 1 st in each back neck CO st, and then pick up and knit 2 sts for every 3 rows along front edge, placing a marker when you reach locking stitch marker. Continue to pick up and knit 2 sts for every 3 rows until you reach Garter Edge, and then pick up and knit 1 st for every 2 rows.

Work even in garter stitch (knit every row) until Band measures 4 in./10 cm, ending with a WS row.

Next row (RS): Knit to m, slm, knit to 1 st before next m, w&t.

Next row (WS): Knit to 1 st before m, w&t.

Next row (RS): Knit to 3 sts before last wrapped st, w&t.

Next row (WS): Knit to 3 sts before last wrapped st, w&t.

Repeat the previous 2 rows 10 more times until you have a total of 12 wrapped sts on each side.

Next row (RS): Knit to end (you do not need to hide your wraps).

Next row (WS): Knit.

BO all sts loosely.

Weave in ends, block, and wear proudly!

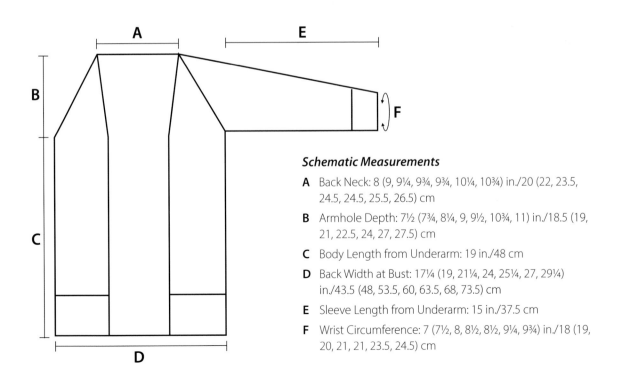

Schematic Measurements

A Back Neck: 8 (9, 9¼, 9¾, 9¾, 10¼, 10¾) in./20 (22, 23.5, 24.5, 24.5, 25.5, 26.5) cm

B Armhole Depth: 7½ (7¾, 8¼, 9, 9½, 10¾, 11) in./18.5 (19, 21, 22.5, 24, 27, 27.5) cm

C Body Length from Underarm: 19 in./48 cm

D Back Width at Bust: 17¼ (19, 21¼, 24, 25¼, 27, 29¼) in./43.5 (48, 53.5, 60, 63.5, 68, 73.5) cm

E Sleeve Length from Underarm: 15 in./37.5 cm

F Wrist Circumference: 7 (7½, 8, 8½, 8½, 9¼, 9¾) in./18 (19, 20, 21, 21, 23.5, 24.5) cm

TUTORIAL: PICKING UP STITCHES ALONG A STOCKINETTE EDGE

1. Starting in the corner of your work with Right Side facing, insert your right-hand needle under both strands of the edge stitch.

2. Wrap yarn and pull a loop through. This is your first picked up stitch.

3. Repeat for the next edge stitch.

4. Skip over the next stitch.

5. Insert your right-hand needle under both strands of the next edge stitch.

6. Continue until you have picked up the number of stitches specified by the pattern.

Acknowledgments

This book would not exist without the support and hard work of several people. First and foremost, I'd like to thank my mom, Leslie Feierstone-Barna, for her constant championing, late-night pep talks, unconditional support, and sample knitting. Thank you also to my dad, Dennis Barna, not just for feeding me home-cooked food but also for raising me to see the world as an artist and to treat all of my endeavors as art.

For this book, I had another opportunity to work with my very favorite knitwear photographer, Gale Zucker. Without her incredible eye, this book would not be what it is. The adorable Randi Nicole Jean, who is not just a model but also an accomplished violinist and IT specialist(!!), modeled several of the patterns.

The photographs for the tutorials were taken by my intrepid boyfriend, Chad Ferber.

Lastly, a huge thank you to my BKFF (best knitting friend forever), Amanda Hinski, for sharing my enthusiasm about new projects and for always responding with "Absolutely!" when I say, "I can get this done by Monday, right?"

Visual Index

Projects

Technicolor Dream Cowl   1

Lilac Leg Warmers   5

Pistachio Baby Blanket   9

Kate's Moss Hat   13

Blue Jay Mitts   17

Summer Storm Shawl   21

Kaaterskill Shawl   26

Abigail Shawl   31

Moonlight Hat   35

Baby Moonlight Hat   39

Hothouse Shawl   43

Mountain Time Mitts   48

Aquarius Cowl   52

Garlic Clove Hat   57

Flint Corn Hat   61

Scrap Blanket   65

Psychic Rainbow Mittens   70

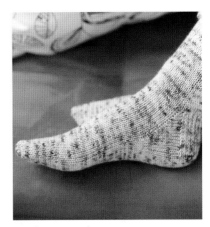

Treehouse Socks   73

A Pointy Reckoning Pullover   79

Bluebird Cardigan   86

Enchanted Wood Cardigan   91

Tutorials

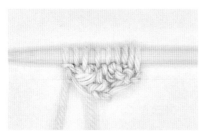

Garter Tab Cast-On   24

A Note on Blocking   30

Picot Bind-Off   46

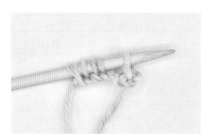

Picot Cast-On   55

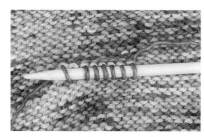

Picking Up Stitches on Inside of Hat   64

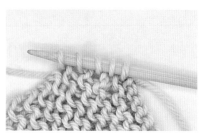

Picking Up Stitches along a Garter Stitch Edge   69

Grafting   77

Short Rows   84

Picking Up Stitches along a Stockinette Edge   96